# DARK TALES
## *of the*
# ENO RIVER

DAVID COOK

THE
History
PRESS

Published by The History Press
Charleston, SC
www.historypress.com

Copyright © 2025 by David Cook
All rights reserved

*Unless otherwise noted, images are courtesy of the author.*

First published 2025

Manufactured in the United States

ISBN 9781467158350

Library of Congress Control Number: 2024947369

*For my wife, Sheila, who was taken by ALS in 2022.*
*The Eno River weaved through most of our life together.*

# CONTENTS

# CONTENTS

CONTENTS

# PREFACE

We know the Eno as a peaceful, beautiful, relaxing river. It is often referred to as the "Tranquil Eno." But hidden around the river bends, in the forested hills and within the communities through which it flows are stories of mystery, mayhem and murder. What follows is a collection of tales from the river's history distant and near. I have tried to be authentic to the facts, but the murkiness of history obscures many details. Most of what we call history now was at the time just considered living and nothing was written down. As such, when necessary, I have presented the stories based on the best preponderance of the evidence. Suffice it to say they came from newspapers, history books, Eno River Association journals and calendars, ranger reports, court records, oral history, maps, obituaries, grave records and personal accounts. When this project started, it was intended for campfire storytelling programs. But as I peered under the rocks and around the river bends, too many stories revealed themselves to be contained in occasional fireside talks; too many people needed to be remembered.

## The River

In northwestern Orange County, North Carolina, two creeks come together: the East and West Forks of the Eno. From there, the river

Eno River at Pleasant Green Access, Eno River State Park.

meanders a crooked thirty-three miles. It begins with a southerly flow, originating in rural farm country and then skirting the community of Efland. Turning east, the Eno pierces the heart of Hillsborough, briefly the colonial capital. Water, terrain and natural resources made it an advantageous place to build a town. Indian villages had occupied this same spot for hundreds of years, the last being the Occaneechi. An Indian trading path intersected the river here. Continuing east, the Eno passes through northern Durham, where tobacco fields have been replaced by suburbs. Then the river meanders into rural eastern Durham County, where it joins another piedmont river, the Flat. The intertwined waters are hence known as the Neuse River.

Most of the land adjacent to the Eno has been conserved in natural forest. The Eno winds through city parks in Hillsborough and Durham. Fifteen miles of the river reside in Eno River State Park and Occoneechee Mountain State Natural Area. Upriver, Duke University has protected lands on the Eno. The lower Eno is federal land, within the Falls Lake flood zone. The Eno River Association holds properties scattered up and down the river in permanent protection. Since 1966, the Association has been the guardian of the Eno in all things natural, historical and cultural.

The Eno is a treasure to Durham and Orange Counties. In 2021, more than one million people visited the two state parks. Hundreds of thousands more visit the city parks. For two days every July, the community comes together in a big celebration of the river at the Festival for the Eno held on the historic campus of West Point on the Eno. Though the waterway is much beloved, most people enjoying the Eno never notice that sometimes the sky turns dark.

# HOOVES, WHEELS AND RAILS

## The Last Ride of John Ray

### *Friday, May 12, 1820*

Stone's Creek is a six-mile tributary of the Eno River. It begins near Hillsborough, heading south to the New Hope community. There it makes an abrupt course change to the northeast, entering the river a short distance upstream from the Pleasant Green Road Bridge.

The Stony Creek community was thriving along Stone's Creek in the 1800s, just four and a half miles southeast of Hillsborough as the crow flies. More will be said about the name discrepancy later. Stony Creek community was growing. Businesses and homes were being built. Seven years after this incident, a U.S. post office was established there. Along with community progress, something insidious was growing. It was alcohol consumption. Drinking was so alarming that for decades, church and civic leaders organized community temperance efforts to curb the sad effects. However, the leaders lamented their lack of success in gaining members to their temperance unions or in curbing consumption.

John C. Ray was a resident of Stony Creek. He had once been a respectable fellow. In 1803, he concluded his duty as a colonel in the North Carolina militia. But that was then, and on this day, seventeen years later, his interests were entertainment, and the entertainment of the day was the hanging of William Sparrow.

Stone Creek at Eno River State Park.

The hanging of William B. "Buck" Sparrow drew a vast concourse of spectators to Hillsborough. Students at the University of North Carolina were given leave of their classes to attend. John Ray and friends made the one-hour ride on horseback from Stony Creek. Buck Sparrow was being executed for shooting in the head and killing, with malicious intent, his hunting companion John Hunt. The murder was accomplished in full view of a witness. No question, a guilty man was going to die, to the delight of the assembled crowd.

It is a wise man who learns from others' mistakes, a foolish man who learns from his own. Sparrow tried to make this point to the crowd gathered below the gallows. In his final words, he warned them about the evils that come from drunkenness. It was in a whiskey-driven fury that he committed murder. They did not listen. The crowd was drinking heavy and Ray among them. Drinking was a common recreation at public hangings.

After the execution, Ray and his friends, as also usual on such occasions, engaged in the dangerous occupation of running their horses. Riding at a full gallop back to Stony Creek, twice Ray fell from his horse and got back on. These were warnings, but he did not pay any mind to them. Getting back on the horse, he again pursued his fate and was hurried into eternity when on his third fall Ray fractured his skull. He lingered overnight, dying early the next morning.

*Stone's Creek takes its name from Edward Stone, through whose 1755 land grant the creek ran to the Eno River. Unaware of the origin of the creek name, newcomers altered the name, supposing it referred to the rocky bottom. Current maps label it Stony Creek, which was also true during Ray's time. However, the John Collet map of North Carolina from 1770 and the Henry Mouzon map of 1775 clearly label the stream Stone's Creek. The Eno River Association has always advocated returning to the earliest known names for natural features and continues to do so for this tributary. You can visit the scenic Stone's Creek at Eno River State Park's Pleasant Green Access and Triangle Land Conservancy's Brumley Nature Preserve; however, both have signs with the later rendition of the name.*

# Rock and Roll Stage

## *Tuesday, July 26, 1853*

Under normal conditions, the Eno is a shallow, quiet river. The water is very clear. But a big rainstorm changes everything. Runoff moves swiftly down the steep hills of the valley, filling the river, which rises and rages, and stirring sediment that turns the water chocolate-milk brown. The swift water is fun for canoes but has the force to move loose boulders. And the boulders affixed to the bottom disappear under the surging obscurity.

The stagecoach running from Raleigh to Greensboro reached the Eno River crossing near Hillsborough about midnight. It carried thirteen passengers plus the stage crew. Moon and lantern light are difficult navigation aids even when you know the crossing, and this driver was unfamiliar with the river and new to this ford. For all he knew, the swollen, swift river was always like this, and he drove the team into the water. They might have made it, but the driver sent the right side of the stage up on a hidden rock. With the conveyance now tilted, the relentless power of the river did the rest, turning the coach over on its side.

A passenger, Dr. J.P. Hall, took charge, directing the men to extricate the women and children. A Hillsborough resident, Mr. Christmas, heard the ruckus and rushed into the river, and together the men escorted all the women and children safely to shore. Miraculously, despite darkness, slippery footing and rushing water, no life was lost or injuries sustained. The mail and most of the baggage were saved. The baggage on top of the stage did come loose and floated downriver. Most of it was recovered, but two trunks were never seen again. As long as they didn't get caught on a tree or rock, it is possible that luggage made it 275 miles to the Pamlico Sound.

The passengers weren't going to the Pamlico for their luggage, so they made their way to the Hillsborough stage house where they were well cared for by a Mr. Nichols, who showed every kindness. Eventually, the stagecoach was retrieved from the river, and everyone continued to Greensboro.

Returning from Greensboro three days later, the same stagecoach, with the same driver, hit the same rock, in the same Eno River ford and turned over again. Three of the same passengers from Tuesday night were in the coach and got dunked again. Once again, no one died, and no one was injured. However, the stage company, in no uncertain terms, charged the driver to never cross the Eno again until someone pointed out that #*$% rock to him.

# No Jumping from the Bridge

## Monday, May 24, 1884

We have all seen the signs prohibiting us from the fun of diving off a bridge into the waters below. Someone should have explained that to Frank Tilley's horse.

Frank and his friend R.A.T. Robertson were out for a ride in in Frank's horse-drawn buggy. This little adventure happened while crossing the Eno River on the Guess Road Bridge. Back then there were no guard rails, and the bridge was twenty feet over the river. Some horses just do not do well on wooden bridges. Something spooked the horse, and it began to back up. Robertson jumped out of the buggy and caught the horse by the bridle, but his attempt to stop the horse failed. In an instant, the buggy went over the edge, throwing Frank out and over the side. The weight of the buggy pulled the horse over the edge and the jerk of the reins drew Robertson in after them.

Frank hit the river first. The buggy fell on Frank, and the horse fell on the buggy. Robertson landed on the horse, and there they were, in one big pile. The river was rocky and shallow, but remarkably neither man nor equine was seriously hurt. The condition of the buggy remains unknown.

Looking down at the Eno from the Guess Road bridge.

# The Lucky Drummer

## *Monday, June 1, 1885*

The train depot at the corner of Nash and Eno Streets in Hillsborough was demolished in the 1970s, but it used to be a hopping place. In 1885, the wooden railroad trestle over the Eno River was less than one hundred yards from the depot. On the night of June 1, a train heading west stopped, and the drummer, riding with the commercial travelers, assumed they were at the platform for the Hillsborough station.

The drummer is what we call a yard conductor today. The drummer would supervise and coordinate the activities of the crew switching railroad cars within the railroad yard. However, this night, the stop was not at the depot as he believed but actually a stop to allow the steam engine to take on water. As the engine filled, the caboose and some passenger cars were parked on the trestle.

The drummer was in a hurry. He was so familiar with the Hillsborough station that he knew he could find his way, even at night. Without looking, he stepped out of the car, suitcase in hand. Stepping from the car's platform, he dropped twenty-six feet into the Eno. Most of the Eno is shallow, with a hard, rocky bottom. He got lucky. In those days, there was a milldam in Hillsborough pooling the water. Here the Eno was ten feet deep, which saved his life. Splashing down like a wood duck out of a tree, the drummer knew how to swim, so other than getting wet and scared, he was fine. In the dark he was disoriented, and it took a bit to get his bearings and figure out where he could climb out of the river. He scrambled up the brushy bank, and if it was like the rest of the Eno, he was grabbing onto poison ivy. He then walked to the station platform, where he reported his narrow escape. Records do not indicate if the suitcase made it with him.

# Lethal Railroad

## Friday, September 26, 1890

Around 8:00 p.m. a construction train on the Lynchburg and Durham Railroad was traveling on the south side of the Eno River through a "cut." A cut is where a deep trench is dug through a hill to lay track, maintaining a low grade, as trains can't handle steep grades. Cuts have high and steep banks on both sides of the track. This situation profoundly set up the incident only seconds away.

The train was running about four miles per hour on straight track passing through the cut when the shanty car (now we call it a caboose) inexplicably jumped off the track and was twisted around and slid up the cut embankment. George Cooper, the cook on the train, was riding the shanty. As the car left the track, he leaped out but chose badly and went out the side in the direction the car was going. As the shanty swung around, he was crushed between the car and embankment, dying a short time later.

H. R. Lee leaped from the shanty car at the same time. He suffered painful but not serious injuries. Another man was asleep in the car in front of the shanty. The screaming and yelling awoke him, and he rushed to the door. He jumped out the car headfirst, striking a rock pile and severely bruising his head and face. The accident could not be attributed to carelessness or neglect, and why the shanty car jumped the track remains a mystery.

*The press coverage of this incident exposed disturbing attitudes in North Carolina society at the time. This terrible accident was reported in at least four newspapers. In three of the four, all of the reporting was straightforward news, and in all four this was true for*

The abandoned Lynchburg and Durham trestle crossing the Eno.

*the description of what happened to George Cooper, a Black man, and H.R. Lee, a White man. But the* Wilmington Morning Star, *in a crass attempt to be humorous, described the ordeal of the third man injured, who was also Black man, in a manner disturbingly degrading of his race.*

## Long Legs and Crossties

### Monday, April 9, 1894

This story really isn't so much about Devereux Turner. You know the fellow. He was Mister Everything in Hillsborough from the 1870s until he moved to South Carolina in 1904. He was a lawyer for decades before becoming a doctor of veterinary surgery. He was a storekeeper, owned a bar over on King Street supported by his distillery two miles east of town, owned the Hillsboro Drug Company with its popular soda fountain and owned the

Hillsborough train trestle. Nowadays, the Riverwalk greenway passes underneath.

Occoneechee Hotel. When he and his wife lived on Churton Street, they sold dairy products out of the house until they moved to West King Street, perhaps to be close to the bar. He was always politically active and got himself elected county treasurer. He made a couple of runs at state senate, but that didn't go anywhere. To top it all off, he was a competitive croquet player. He owned a heck of lot of land in and around Hillsborough, but after he moved to South Carolina he lost 201 acres of it in a lawsuit involving horses. But this story isn't so much about Devereux, it's more about his horse.

Devereux Turner hitched his horse to his wagon and drove over to the Hillsborough Train Depot, there on the corner of Nash and Eno Streets. He parked the horse and wagon expecting them to stay put, but you never know what's going on in a horse's head. Someone nearby cranked up a hand organ, and the horse did not like it. The horse spooked and ran away as fast as he could, pulling the wagon with Devereux running after. The horse took off down the railroad track and kept going until he reached the middle of the iron bridge over the Eno River. Here, Devereux's day went from vexing to chaos. The horse's hooves slipped between the bridge crossties and dropped through the spacings. The scared equine was stuck with his belly on the bridge, legs dangling over the river, wagon still hitched to the horse.

It took a lot of time and a lot of work to get that horse off the bridge. Trains were coming, adding pressure to their conundrum. The wagon had to be unhitched, backed off the bridge and lifted off the track. This took a lot of manpower. But what was really hard was getting the legs of a scared horse up from between the crossties and then leading him off the bridge without panicking and going off the side, perhaps taking the rescuers over simultaneously. With patience and determination, the rescue succeeded. Remarkably, the horse showed no sign of injury except some skinned places, and the wagon's only wound was a broken shaft.

## Train Trestle Turns Terminal

### *Friday, August 19, 1904*

About six o'clock in the evening, eighteen-year-old Jo Flintall was walking the train trestle over the Eno River in Hillsborough. Bridges across the Eno were few and far between. For many people, the train trestle was the shortest way to cross. Just east of the bridge was a sharp curve in the track, and an approaching train cannot be seen but for only a short distance. You had to rely on hearing to know when it was safe to cross. It is presumed Jo did not hear the train until he was halfway across the bridge with nowhere to escape. It was a work train bearing down on him. The engine struck and sent him hurling off the bridge into the river. The crew on board got the train stopped and went back and got Jo out of the river. He was hurt bad. They carried him to the nearby Hillsborough Railroad Depot, where he died moments later.

## Hard Luck Bridge

### *Saturday, November 18, 1905*

The iron train trestle over the Eno in Hillsborough had its share of disaster—some tragic, others just spectacular. About 3:30 p.m., Southern Railway Freight Train No. 172 was crossing the bridge; 172 was considered a fast freight train. The engine and forward cars made it across safely. Can't say the same about the twelve cars in the middle. Loaded mainly with lumber and fabrics, those freight cars derailed and crashed in wild abandon. One car was flung fifty feet down the steep embankment and landed in the river. Another car swung around and lay crossways on the bridge with the tracks holding one end and the other end hanging out over the river. Six freight cars went down the embankment and were badly damaged. The last four didn't make it to the bridge and were off the side of the tracks. Lumber and fabrics were scattered on the banks and floating in the water. Somehow the caboose managed to stay on the track. The crew was in the forward cars and the caboose, so there was no loss of life or injury. Rail ties and tracks were torn up for more than one hundred feet.

The Southern Railway Company was claiming they would have the car caught across the bridge removed and repairs to the bridge done by the end of the next day. Observers in Hillsborough expected Southern was full of it and getting that car off and repairing the bridge was going to take a whole lot longer. Since the other cars left the track, cleanup was necessary, but they weren't blocking traffic. Reality was it took days before trains could pass. East and westbound trains coming in that afternoon stopped on either side of the trestle and swapped passengers and then returned from whence they came. Investigation determined a broken flange on a car wheel caused the derailment.

*I found seven wrecks and tragedies on the various Hillsborough train trestles between 1885 and 1950. There may be more I did not find.*

# The 174 Disaster

## Friday, May 8, 1914

It was eleven o'clock on a Friday night and the Southern Railway eastbound freight train No. 174 was chugging about thirty miles an hour through Hazel's Cut, down a steep grade. A group of Alamance County boys were "hoboing" their way to Hillsborough (sneaking a ride on the train) to attend a Saturday baseball game. Three boys were from Haw River: Will Powell, Carlyle Way and Bernice Prince. Three boys hailed from Graham: Edgar Morris, Arthur Griffin and Tim Stevens. Joining them was Bryan Stout from Burlington. Four of them were riding on a loaded lumber car.

The site of the 174 disaster.

The train was approaching the Eno River bridge about two miles west of Hillsborough, the one closer to Efland. Without warning, most of the train jumped the rails and crumpled into massive wreckage. The engine and tender (fuel car for a steam engine) popped loose and remained on the track. But their brakes failed, and they couldn't stop until after they crossed the bridge and reached Hillsborough. The caboose also managed to stay on the tracks. Twenty-three cars in between were smashed into firewood kindling. The property damage was tremendous. A Southern Railway claim agent said it was the worst he had ever seen. Several large tanks containing crude oil were among the wrecked cars. Oil was standing in pools and flowing down a drain into the river, forming a black slick completely covering the river all the way to Dimmock's Mill. Seventy-five yards of track were twisted and loose and would never serve the railroad again. One car near the front caught on a steel rail and was forced from the track, carrying the rail with it and bending the rail forty-five degrees. The damage paled in comparison to what happened to the ball game–bound boys.

Edgar and Carlyle were severely injured. They were transported home to their family farms for extensive recuperation under doctor's care. Will,

Bryan and Tim were hurt, in serious condition and taken home, but their injuries were not life-threatening. Arthur and Bernice were missing.

Nine hours later, a Saturday morning train coming from the west had to stop at the wreck site. Old soldiers returning to Hillsborough from a reunion got out and walked the rest of the way. Passengers heading toward the coast walked to the Hillsborough depot, where they were put on a train that would have been heading west but reversed course and took them to Goldsboro.

All day Saturday, a wrecking crew from Greensboro was on the scene hoisting derailed cars and clearing wreckage. Getting the track open was helped by the location up on an embankment. A work train with a derrick cleared the track by throwing trucks, cars and tanks down the bank. The worst fears came to pass in the morning while moving the devastated lumber car. Arthur Griffin and Bernice Prince were uncovered in the pile, dead right there.

In the ensuing days, speculation grew that No. 174's brakes had been tampered with, but this was not proven. The dead were buried on Sunday, May 10, 1914.

# Kate's Final Steps of Kindness

## *Wednesday, July 22, 1931*

It was four o'clock on a Wednesday afternoon and sixty-nine-year-old Kate Plott was bringing groceries to a neighbor who was very ill with cancer. Leaving the grocery store in Hillsborough, Kate took the shortest route, which in those days meant walking across the Eno River on the railroad trestle. Something must have had her distracted, as she failed to hear the Southern Railway train bearing down on her. When she realized it, she couldn't run fast enough. The train struck and killed her instantly. Her body was horribly mangled. It was an unfair end to an angel of mercy. She was survived by her husband, Thomas, and a daughter who lived all the way to Arkansas. Walker Funeral Home took care of the body, and she was laid to rest in Linwood Cemetery in Graham, North Carolina.

*The* News and Observer *reported Kate's last name as Clapp, but it was Plott. She shares a grave with her husband, who passed just two years after she did.*

# Why Were You on This Track?

## *Saturday, February 11, 1950*

The Eno Cotton Mill sits on the north bank of the Eno River in West Hillsborough. It had to be close to the river to draw water for mill operation and to dump waste. The train trestle across the river is just 450 yards downstream, and the track parallels the river.

Margaret Louise Sloan was an Eno Cotton Mills employee. She was twenty-four years old. Raymond Richard Dixon was eleven years her senior and a World War II veteran. He was a former Eno Cotton Mills employee and now worked at Erwin Mills in Durham. Both of them had parents and brothers living in Hillsborough.

Just past midnight, Margaret and Raymond were walking the railroad track, about one hundred feet from the Eno River trestle. This is on the north side of the river, between the mill and the river crossing. We don't know why they were on the track or why so late at night. We know the time because we know when the westbound Southern Railway freight train No. 255 passed that spot, striking and killing them, although no one on the train realized it at the time. About seven o'clock the next morning, Charlie Crabtree found their badly mutilated bodies.

Coroner H. J. Walker and Sheriff Sam Latta investigated and ruled an inquest unnecessary. They believed the two were killed accidentally when standing or sitting on the track. They had no theory of how this could have happened. It leaves us with questions. Was this an accident? Or was it something more? Perhaps a suicide or a murder/suicide? How could they not know a freight train was bearing down on them? The answers died just after midnight.

Margaret's funeral was held on Sunday at the West Hillsborough Methodist Church. Burial followed at Cedar Hill Cemetery, also known as Erwin Mills Cemetery in Durham. The cemetery, built for employees

Margaret Sloan is in an abandoned graveyard, but someone comes by.

of Erwin Mills, is down a lonely, dusty road, where it is overgrown and abandoned. Margaret's tombstone is still there. It broke off the base and for many years lay flat on the ground. But when I visited it in the winter of 2023, someone had set the stone upright and placed flowers on the grave. The epitaph reads "Blessed Are the Pure in Heart." The Sloan family had known a lot of heartache. Six of Margaret's nine siblings did not live past the age of three. Raymond's funeral was in the same church, three hours after Margaret's. He was buried in the town cemetery. Oddly, though, his date of departure is inscribed one year and one day earlier on his tombstone.

*Eno Cotton Mills closed down in 1984. Now the buildings house a variety of businesses, arts and a charter school. Occoneechee Mountain State Natural Area and Gold Park are on land once owned by the mill.*

# Red Mill Takes Three Souls

## Friday, September 11, 1970

Friday night late, after dark, a single car carrying five teenagers was traveling Red Mill Road. For a reason we may never know, as the car crossed the bridge over the Eno, it veered to the side and plunged into the river to rest on the muddy bottom twelve feet deep. Wayne Ellis and Lauron Webber managed to extricate themselves out as the car was sinking. But try as they could, in the deep water the doors would not open to release their friends. Those two made it to safety. The other three left their lives at the bottom of the river. The bodies were found in the car when it was recovered.

Three families and the community around northeastern Durham and southern Person Counties were in grief. The three who drowned that night were:

Lee Roy Ellis, age nineteen, from Bahama. He worked for the state highway commission. He is buried at Ellis Chapel Methodist Church, and his nickname, "Hot Rod," is inscribed on his tombstone.

William Ralph Clements, age seventeen, from Bahama. He was a Northern High School senior. At Woodlawn Memorial Park, the inscription on his grave marker reads, "We Loved Him a Lot but God Loved Him More."

Red Mill Bridge over the Eno.

Thomas Earl Carter, age sixteen from Rougemont. He was a sophomore at Person High School. He was also buried at Ellis Chapel, and the inscription on his stone carries the sincere sentiment "Gone But Not Forgotten."

*Some news reported this tragedy occurred in the Neuse River. However, the Red Mill Road Bridge is more than a mile upstream from the confluence of the Eno and Flat Rivers where the Neuse proper begins.*

# Too Fast, Too Far

## *Saturday, March 23, 1985*

Driving north on Guess Road, heading downhill way too fast, nineteen-year-old Timothy Clark was driving his 1976 Chevrolet Camaro. Clark lived just around the corner on Rose of Sharon Church Road. In the passenger seat was fifteen-year-old Tammy Graves from Durham, a ninth-grader at Carrington Junior High School. At 12:26 p.m., as they reached the Eno River, the Camaro veered and ran off the left side of the road. It hit the bridge and went airborne. Flying eighty-nine feet and dropping twenty, the

Tammy and Timothy landed on the far bank.

car clipped off treetops before landing upside down on the other side of the river on rocky, dry riverbed.

Graves was ejected from the car in flight. She landed on top of the upside-down car. Clark was trapped inside the car for more than an hour until the Lebanon Volunteer Fire Department cut him out. The car was demolished. Both teens were rushed to Durham County General Hospital, where they were placed in intensive care in critical condition. By Monday morning, Clark's condition had been upgraded to fair, but he spent more days in the hospital. Graves lingered in critical condition for nine days until she perished. Her funeral was held on April 3, and she is buried in Oak Grove Memorial Gardens in Durham County.

*The riverbed where Clark and Graves landed was just down the hill from the old cinder block building called the White House, the first office of the Eno River Association, leased from the state park. The building is still there but not fit for habitation. At the time, this was a narrow two-lane bridge, not the modern five-lane divided highway single-span bridge we have today.*

## 2

# MURDER AND OTHER UNLAWFUL ABERRATIONS

## Atrocity Heretofore Unknown

### Tuesday, September 12, 1837

The biggest plantation on the Eno was also the biggest plantation in North Carolina. The Cameron Plantation, at more than thirty thousand acres, extended from the Eno to the Little, Flat and Neuse Rivers in what is now eastern Durham County.

It was a Tuesday. That in itself was unusual. The normal routine of Thomas A. Cameron was to ride horseback to Stagville to visit his father every Friday and return home to Raleigh on Monday. Thomas was the oldest son of the Honorable Duncan Cameron, owner of the Cameron Plantation. Thomas, then thirty-one years old, was described as suffering a physical weakness and having learning disabilities. This may be why sixteen years later his younger brother Paul would inherit the plantation. Paul Cameron went on to become the richest man in North Carolina. Today we can visit remnants of the Cameron Plantation at Stagville State Historic Site, Penny's Bend Nature Preserve and Horton Grove Nature Preserve.

On this particular day, Thomas was riding the Lower Hillsboro Road, eleven miles from Raleigh. Midmorning he stopped his horse to reach for ripe muscadine grapes dangling from the trees. As he stretched out, his left arm partially shielded his face. Nothing alerted him to the evil concealed in the bushes on the left side of the road until that first gun blast roared in his ears. One shot hit his temple, another his nose. A shot hit his neck. Several hit his face. The left arm raised beside his head took nine bullets.

The startled horse took off running. Thomas managed to stay in the saddle for several hundred yards, where he met a party of laborers responding to the sound of shots and calls for help. The men gave him aid and helped him back to the plantation. The *Weekly Standard* newspaper of Raleigh reported that Thomas's wounds were not life-threatening, and he was expected to recover. Apparently, he did, because we know he was still alive for his father's funeral in 1853. An investigation determined the gun was loaded with bluster shot and slugs. This meant each shot carried multiple pellets. The nine shots in his arm were probably one shotgun blast. Evidence at the scene indicated the assailant had been lying in wait in the bushes since Monday, probably expecting Thomas to return home per his normal routine.

The *Weekly Standard* commented further: the motive on a "peaceable and non-offending citizen must have been plunder....A case of atrocity heretofore unknown in the history of North Carolina." No record indicating the identification or capture of the perpetrator has surfaced.

# Escape to the River

## *Thursday, March 1, 1917*

On the first day of March, the Hendersons and various farmhands were at work on the family plantation, about a half-mile west of Carrboro. Ten-year-old Alice Henderson left on foot about two o'clock in the afternoon, walking a country road. Alice lived with her grandfather Pink Henderson, a prominent and wealthy farmer. On this day Pink was away on business in Durham.

Charles Atwater was one of the hands working the farm. Except he wasn't Charles Atwater. That was the name he gave the Hendersons. His real name was Charlie Hill, and he was an escaped convict. Weeks earlier he had slipped away from a road crew right there in Orange County while serving a four-month sentence for larceny, convicted in Chatham County Superior Court. He also had done his share of time working Wake County roads for stealing money. The real shame was he was just a teenager. Reports of the day put him at anywhere from sixteen to nineteen years old. On this day, the Hendersons had him cutting firewood.

As Alice walked along unaware, Charlie Hill intercepted her in a lonely spot. Hill grabbed her and rammed his cap into Alice's mouth, but struggling to break free, she was able to yank it out. He choked her, bruising her neck. Alice went to screaming, and relatives came running as Hill was disappearing into the woods. It was a plantation employee, Ed Myrick, who got there first, arriving in time to see Hill fleeing. Alice still held the man's cap; she was terribly frightened and described as in a highly nervous condition.

Deputy Sheriff Will Parker was the first law officer to be notified. Soon officers and armed groups of farmers organized to search for Hill. Going well after dark, an armed posse tracked Hill to the Eno River. Here the trail went cold. It is probable the fleeing man waded into the river to hide his tracks. Neither officers nor citizens gave up the hunt. Excitement and anger were running high in the county. In those times, the sentiments were especially stoked because Hill was a Black man and Alice was a White girl.

The next day, the populace was so worked up that James Purifoy got quite a scare. He was walking to Durham from Chapel Hill. When he got to Durham, plainclothes police officers arrested him under suspicion of committing the assault. Their only evidence was a vague description and blood on his clothes. He didn't get out of jail until the real Hill was brought in the next day.

Hill was found and caught by Deputy Parker about one o'clock in the morning on Saturday, March 3, with the assistance of Special Deputy McCauley from Chapel Hill and Constable Carson of Chatham County. They found him in the Jones Grove area of northern Chatham County, where Hill was at a home playing cards like nothing had happened. Hill didn't resist, and he was taken to Carrboro by motor car. This was 1917, and riding in a motor car was a rare luxury, but it's doubtful Charlie Hill saw it that way.

A preliminary hearing was held at eight o'clock that morning, and Hill was put under a $500 bond (almost $11,000 in today's money). At this time, Alice positively identified him as her assailant, and besides, they had his hat. From the hearing, Hill was rushed to Durham for safekeeping, as there was fear that local fury could lead to vigilante justice.

When he was interviewed at the Durham jail, this was Hill's first response: He had not talked to or touched Alice. No explanation given as to how she had his hat or the bruises on her neck. Then, after first saying he had not talked to her, he admitted being on the plantation with Alice and said she came to him and asked him to get some grapevines for her. Hill said he then started to her home with her and met a White man who told him not to come to the house so he left for Chatham County. When asked why he ran away when Ed Myrick arrived on the scene, he said Myrick threatened to kill him with a rock so he fled. But he couldn't explain how he saw Myrick if he had already left for Chatham County.

That night, Hill was sent by train back to Hillsborough and jailed under the guard of Deputy Sheriff Thomas Sparrow and two deputized citizens. On the ride, he was still asserting his innocence. Durham authorities protested the return to Orange County, as the Hillsborough jail was one of the oldest in North Carolina, poorly constructed and would not stand up to a mob. Durham officers advised it was dangerous to return him as a Black man who allegedly assaulted a White girl. Numerous lynching threats were reported. However, returned he was, and Orange County deputies were diligent in guarding the jail, protecting Hill from reprisals.

One week after the assault, Alice's grandfather Pink Henderson died suddenly. Initially, it was presumed stress over the attack on his granddaughter was the cause. However, his doctor in Chapel Hill determined the death was natural and not related to the incident. Alice went on to live with other relatives.

On April 4, 1917, just over a month from the assault, Charlie Hill was sentenced to ten years in the Hillsborough penitentiary.

# Fatal Whiskey

## *Saturday, December 10, 1921*

Samuel Douglas went by his middle name, "Gattis." He was twenty-seven years old, and he and his new wife, May, had a young daughter and were expecting a baby. They lived with his father in an unpainted house with lap board siding out on Pleasant Green Road. He was popular, and his name appeared on the guest list of many west Durham social gatherings. He was an active member at Pleasant Green Church. He was also a World War I veteran, just three years back from the war to end all wars. And Gattis Douglas was a distiller of illicit spirits.

It was early in the Christmas season. Prohibition enforcement officer C.G. Rosemond was working with county officers from Durham and Orange

Gattis Douglas rests in the Pleasant Green Methodist Church cemetery.

looking for illegal whiskey stills. Rosemond was a prolific detector of moonshining and must have had an informant. He went through one ninety-day period where he averaged capturing one still a day, mostly in Orange County. Late Saturday afternoon, they were slipping up on an operation a short distance downstream of the Durham Water Works station on the Eno River. When they reached the still, it was in full operation with three blockaders (still operators) present. The officers made their move, and the blockaders tried to run upriver. Just past the water pumping station dam, their terrestrial escape was cut off so they took the last route open and plunged into the deep water of the winter river.

Two succeeded in reaching the opposite bank and escaped through forest and brush. As the officers watched, it was apparent the last man either could not swim or wasn't trying. After he went under twice, they rescued him and brought him back to shore. They identified him as Gattis Douglas, and he was hurting bad from the cold. The water in the Eno reflects the air temperature, and on this December day it was bitter. Gattis was turning blue, and the officers took him back to the still, where the fire was burning, and sat him there for quite a while to warm up and dry his clothes. Then, showing remarkable compassion, they took him home, allowing him to go to his room to change clothes before being taken to a federal commissioner for arraignment.

Only a moment had passed as the officers waited when they heard the gunshot. Rushing into the bedroom, they found Gattis with a terrible wound to his chest from the shotgun laying nearby. Officers rushed to west Durham and brought back a doctor. Upon examination, the doctor determined there was no hope Gattis would survive. The doctor and officers who saw the massive wound couldn't understand why he didn't die right away. As it was, Gattis lingered until the evening of the next day. Seventeen-year-old neighbor Clyde Walker came to the house to help clean the body. He said Gattis had enough lead shot in him that it rattled when they rolled him over. Officer Rosemond said it was the first time he ever had someone take their own life after being caught at a still.

*Top*: The old Durham Water Works Pump Station dam abutted this rock outcrop. Today, hikers cross over it on the Dunnagan Trail.

*Bottom*: Across the river, the dam joined the pump building of the waterworks. Stone walls still stand.

Gattis Douglas was laid to rest at Pleasant Green Methodist Church. His epitaph reads, "Fond Memory Clings to Thee." We are left with wondering. Was the prospect of jail so devastating that Gattis would rather end it all and leave his family? When he was surrounded by uniformed men with guns, did the demons of war rear their ugly head? Or perhaps, as some family speculated, as an active church member was the embarrassment of being caught moonshining too much for him?

While a tragedy that May would never want to endure, her life in the Pleasant Green Community went on. Douglas Junior "Buddy" was born four months later. Like his father, he served his country in the U.S. Army. This time it was the Second World War. May did remarry and had two more children, including another son, Ted, who went on to be a successful local cattle farmer and one of the oldest members of the church where Gattis Douglas lays.

*Serving in World War I for most meant witnessing horrific violence. Today we would recognize the psychological effects as post-traumatic stress syndrome in need of treatment. In 1921, a soldier would be expected to just "get over it." Perhaps Gattis Douglas's capture set off a storm in his mind that he could not handle. Newspaper reports had his home on Cole Mill Road, but consulting with descendants, the Douglas house was on nearby Pleasant Green Road, where is now the entrance to Pleasant Green Estates. The house stood until 1972. You can visit the site of Gattis Douglas's capture at the Pump Station Access of Eno River State Park.*

# The Drownings of Bud Cain

## Monday, September 29–Wednesday, October 1, 1924

In a desperate attempt to escape from Deputy George King, longtime moonshiner Bud Cain took off running with a sack containing two gallons of moonshine liquor slung over his shoulder. He tried to wade the rain-swollen Eno River but tripped in the water on brush hidden below the murky surface. Cain plunged headlong into the swift currents, which carried him into water over twenty feet deep. (Or so the newspapers reported. There is no place in the Eno that deep.) Then Bud Cain disappeared from sight. King saw him go under and never saw him come up. The officer had a clear view for over one hundred yards in each direction and never saw the bootlegger bob up from the water. He had to believe Cain went to his death amid the debris washing along in the muddy torrents.

The next day, Deputy King, along with some other deputies, set out in search of illegal booze. They were riding in a brand-new car of the "Lizzie" type along the slippery, muddy Oxford Road (now called Old Oxford Highway and paved). Late in the day, as they drove up on the Eno River bridge, they saw Bud Cain trudging along the side of the road! Cain's back was bent under the weight of another heavy sack he carried over his shoulder. The deputies drove past him and stopped a few yards ahead of him. As soon as Deputy King stepped out of the car, Cain recognized him, ran for the river and jumped back in. The officers had a full view of the river, and once again, Cain disappeared.

The following day, Wednesday, and who shows up in recorder's court but Bud Cain. He was there to plead not guilty to illegal possession of liquor. Cain was found guilty and sentenced to six months in the Durham jail, to which he appealed his conviction. How Cain escaped the river each time he fell/jumped in remains a mystery, as he wasn't talking.

*Durham law enforcement knew Bud Cain well. He was found guilty of larceny in 1896, was in jail for who knows what in 1898. Robbed a blind man in 1905. Was attacked by Joe Scarborough, who came at him with a gun and knife in 1908. Also, in 1908, Cain was convicted of whipping his wife. These were just the incidents that made the newspaper.*

The deep Kitchen Hole below the Old Oxford Highway Bridge is popular for fishing and swimming.

# Disturbing Discovery

## Monday, April 26, 1926

A Mr. Davis of Danville, Virginia, was fishing the Eno River about 11:00 a.m. near Hillsborough when he made a gruesome discovery. He found a man's body. One foot was caught on a limb. The rest was in the water. Orange County sheriff Bunn Lloyd investigated. The man appeared to be about sixty years old. He had been shot in the left side of his chest with a shotgun. The coroner estimated death occurred two to three weeks earlier. In the dead man's pockets were $2.81 and a note asking for the address for a car sale, but the names on the note were indecipherable. Decomposition was so bad the county buried the body the same day, about two miles from town. The man was never identified and the mystery of his murder never solved.

# Slashed

## Sunday, June 29, 1930

Leroy Medlin and Aubrey Goss were lifelong friends and business partners. They got in a lot of mischief, both together and independently. This incident happened when they were seventeen years old. I can tell you from a lot of experience as a ranger, seventeen years is the prime age for getting in trouble on the Eno.

Leroy and Aubrey went to the Eno with a group of friends for a Sunday swim. They got into an argument with another group at the same spot. There is no record of who started it or what it was about. But it escalated when Leroy was in the river, and a man he didn't know accused him of stepping on his shirt. That man jumped in the water and attacked Leroy with a knife, slashing him in the throat. Aubrey jumped in to save Leroy, and the man turned on him, giving him an ugly gash on his arm. The man then fled the river and the scene.

Durham County sheriff Belvin and his deputies responded, but the attacker was long gone by the time they arrived. They interviewed everyone still there and planned to investigate further. But no arrest was ever made.

Leroy and Aubrey were treated at Watts Hospital. The lacerations proved not to be serious, and the boys were quickly discharged.

*This day on the river, Aubrey Goss and Leroy Medlin were the victims, though we don't know if they instigated anything. However, their penchant for being in the middle of trouble continued for a long time, and Durham law enforcement got to know them well. In 1934, Medlin was arrested and held without bond in the beating and robbery of a woman hitchhiking in Durham. In 1935, Medlin and Goss owned a Durham gas station together. A liquor raid across the road netted 40 gallons of untaxed liquor. Shortly thereafter, both of them were arrested on a plot to attack a man. Their motive was the belief he was the stool pigeon that led to the liquor raid. The same year, Goss was caught with 104 gallons of illegal liquor in his Durham home. In 1938, the pair pleaded guilty in Durham to defrauding the federal government of liquor taxes. They were part of a ring running "monkey rum" from down east to sell in Durham. It was a million-dollar operation with more than one hundred trips and hundreds of thousands of gallons. Goss was considered the ringleader. In 1944, Goss, at the age of thirty-one, was shot in the chest by an ABC agent and was in critical condition but did survive. Leroy Medlin and Aubrey Goss were colorful characters in Durham history.*

# The Hailey Disappearance

## Friday, February 25–Saturday, July 30, 1938

The disappearance of Lillian Hailey in 1938 had Durham buzzing and received extensive press coverage. She disappeared from her Lincoln Avenue home on February 25. But nobody did anything about it until her sister Mary Woodard, another Durhamite, became worried about Lillian's long absence and went to High Sheriff Cat Belvin. The sheriff started a search and investigation on March 17. As evidence mounted, Lillian's husband, William David Hailey, was arrested on suspicion of foul play. Ten days into the investigation, the sheriff stated his opinion to reporters that Lillian likely was the victim of nefarious activity. Belvin sent her description to every police agency and coroner in North Carolina.

William David's story was his wife had gone to Michigan to visit her brother Ira Alston. Sheriff Belvin wired Alston, who replied that Lillian was not there and he knew of no plans for her to travel to Michigan. Her sister Mary didn't know of any such plans either. A search of her home found all her clothing, her wristwatch, her suitcase and a trunk. The only thing missing were the clothes she was wearing when last seen. William David said she didn't take any clothes because she bought a new outfit for the trip. She also left her 1936 model automobile (fully paid for), fifty-five dollars in the bank and the home she owned. Nothing seemed consistent for someone to pick up and leave.

Co-workers at Liggett and Myers Tobacco said she stopped for no purchases and did not mention a trip when Lillian rode home with them the night before she disappeared. Investigation discovered her last paycheck was cashed the day after she disappeared, and the endorsement did not match her signature. Too much time had passed for anyone at the bank to remember who cashed her check. Hundreds of Durham residents volunteered to search places around town where a body could be hidden. The grounds around her home, the cellar and the floor of the garage were dug up in the search. Her brother Alston arrived from Michigan on March 28. His statement was unchanged. His sister had not visited him, and he feared she met with foul play. William David, still in county jail, continued to insist Lillian went to visit her brother. Alston and his sister Mary Woodard, suspicious of William David, took legal action to appoint Mary's husband as guardian of Lillian's estate.

By mid-April, with investigative leads exhausted and insufficient evidence, Lillian's husband had been released from jail. Nothing else happened for three and a half months.

The afternoon of July 30, a Saturday, Harvey Schumake and Walter Johnson, who were neighbors over on Dowd Street in Durham, were bank fishing the Eno River about three hundred yards downstream from the Norfolk and Western Railroad trestle. The river was swollen and swift from recent thunderstorms. Across the river, they saw a body floating in the current, bobbing in the whitewater. They followed the body for almost a mile, and when it floated close to their side, they attempted to snag and retrieve it. They got close enough to identify it was a body, but it was so covered with mud they could not determine race or sex. The size told them it was an adult. Despite their sincere efforts, the river carried the body out of sight.

Giving up, they notified local residents and then went to Durham to report to the sheriff. The locals were first to come out and continue the search. Sheriff Belvin got the report in the late afternoon and determined it was too late in the day to join in. The following morning, the sheriff, deputies, numerous volunteers and local neighbors were out early and searched throughout the day. Continuing into a third day, Sheriff Belvin publicly broached his opinion that the body seen by the fishermen could be Lillian Hailey, as she currently was the only person missing in Durham County.

The sheriff speculated the body had been buried near the river and was uncovered during heavy rains when the river came out of its banks. Those desolate regions of the county where the body was seen were ideal for hiding someone. That the body was covered with muck lent credence to his theory it had been buried. To aid the search, people living along the Eno and Neuse were notified to watch. By August 2, Sheriff Belvin believed the body could have washed as far as Wake County, if it didn't get stuck. Doubt began to creep into his mind as to whether the body could be Lillian. He considered that given the length of time, the body would have decomposed much more, unless the soil slowed the decomposition. He consulted experts, who revealed the body could have been preserved enough underground to still be intact. The sheriff also realized if it wasn't Lillian, it meant someone from outside the local area would have had to have brought a body to the river and buried it, as no one else was missing.

A year after the search began, the Durham newspapers were still covering the disappearance. The mysterious floating body was never found. Lillian Hailey never returned. Mr. Woodward retained care of her property until seven years passed and she could be declared dead. The estate would end up going to her heirs, brother Ira, sister Mary and husband William David, who was still in Durham, having moved to Pettigrew Street.

# Didn't Think to Remove the Tag

## Monday and Tuesday, September 30–October 1, 1957

On Monday night, the Altvater family summer cabin was broken into and robbed. This was their cabin on the Eno River north of Hillsborough. Ann Altvater, a Duke University student, had been there just hours before to store some clothes. Women's apparel worth $500, bed clothing and a power lawn mower were stolen.

Tuesday night, Paul Roberts and Bill Mitchell were playing setback at the Forrest cabin on the Eno northwest of Hillsborough. It was a typical quiet evening of card playing until Joseph "Bill" Stallings and Howard Duncan burst in pointing a .38 special and a hooked tobacco knife. Their faces were covered with ladies' stockings, and their demands were larcenous. They demanded money, taking $400. It was a fiasco of a robbery from the get-go. Roberts and Mitchell recognized both robbers.

The old family summer cabins, once popular on the Eno, have mostly disintegrated, except the O'Briant Cabin maintained at Eno River State Park.

In fact, Howard Duncan had worked for Roberts as a bulldozer operator. When Stallings and Duncan drove off, Roberts and Mitchell gave chase in their car.

As the chase extended to the Eastwood community (as the name implies, east of Hillsborough), the thieves lost control of their 1955 Ford, drove through the fence of the Jones pasture on Crawford Road and wrecked the car. Roberts and Mitchell held their robbers at bay until the police arrived. The thieves were captured and money recovered. The money and the gun had been thrown down in the pasture but weren't hard to find. Stallings and Duncan were in jail a half hour after the robbery, offering no resistance to the officers. The stocking masks were confiscated as evidence. Lo and behold, one of the stockings had a laundry tag identifying the owner. It was from the Altvater burglary the day before.

Stallings and Duncan were bound over to superior court in Orange County, where they pleaded not guilty and were placed on $4,000 bond each. The back-to-back cabin invasions were not Howard Duncan's last criminal adventure on the Eno. In 1961, he was caught after first stealing dynamite from the Hillsborough Prison Camp, then stealing blasting caps and gasoline from the Bacon rock quarry, the same Bacon Quarry that became part of Eno River State Park in 2018. The next step was breaking into the Efland Mill and blowing open the safe, which led to his inevitable arrest. In November 1961, Duncan was sentenced to twenty-three years in state prison.

*West Hillsborough native Howard Duncan's criminal record was extensive. Between 1945 and 1961, he was arrested for secret assault, manslaughter in the death of two men in a truck accident, larceny four times, receiving stolen goods twice, assault with a deadly weapon, breaking and entering twice, affray twice, burglary and armed robbery.*

*Bill Stallings, also from west Hillsborough, committed his fair share. Between 1949 and 1957, he was arrested for fighting three times, assault on an officer, resisting arrest, public drunkenness four times, affray, possession of non-tax paid liquor, drunk and disorderly, burglary and armed robbery.*

# The Eno's Greatest Mystery

## *Friday, February 12, 1971, until now*

Ann Zener and Marion Sands were stalwarts of the Eno River Association. Ann was in the small group that first met to protest the damming of the river. They met in her cottage on a high, steep, mountain laurel–covered bluff that led down to a swimming hole in the Eno called Drowning Horse Pond. She owned over sixty acres with a lot of river frontage and sold all but a small piece around the cottage to Eno River State Park twenty-five years after this tale. Marion Sands was a decades-long volunteer to the mission of saving the Eno, spending many long hours laboring for the cause. Marion lived in the old family home on Howe Street, and her property backed up to Ann's. Their common property line is now the boundary of the Cabelands Access of Eno River State Park.

This story is not about Ann and Marion. It's about what happened on their shared property line. It's the story of the Eno's greatest mystery.

In 1971, there was a dirt road that went straight back from Howe Street, north toward the river through deep pine woods. This road was on the line between the Sands and Zener property ,and the road had a name combining their two surnames, Sanzene Road. The road ended in a clearing about 250 yards from the Eno, where the forest changed to older hardwood. On Thursday, February 25, about 1:00 p.m., surveyor Robert Kirby dropped the cable gate across Sanzene Road and drove back to the clearing, turned

The end of the old Sanzene Road, where trees were the only witnesses to the events of February 1971, and they aren't talking.

around and parked. The day was overcast and gray, about forty degrees. He was there looking for a corner marker between the Zener and Sands property. As Kirby exited his car, he thought he saw a mannequin. There was a leg that could be seen, sticking up outside a pile of leaves. When Kirby got closer, he realized it was an actual human leg. Not totally convinced of what he was seeing, he went back to his car, got a surveyor's stick and went back and poked the leg to assure himself it was real. But we have come in at the middle of the story. We need to go back nearly two weeks to the beginning, on Friday, February 12, 1971.

That winter Friday there had been a misty drizzle all day. Patricia Ann Mann and her boyfriend Jesse McBane did not care. They were getting ready for the Valentine's Dance at Watts Hospital in Durham. Twenty-year-old Patricia was a student at the Watts School of Nursing and lived in a dormitory on the hospital campus. Jesse was a nineteen-year-old North Carolina State University freshman from Chatham County. Jesse was so excited about the dance that he bought a box of candy for Patricia before he even knew if he had transportation to Durham. He and his brother shared a 1968 Ford, and Jesse wasn't supposed to have it that night. It wasn't his turn. He made a deal with his brother, traded days and at the last minute got the car. He called Patricia, and they got to go to the dance. Jesse left so fast he forgot the candy.

The last time they were seen was 11:30 that night when Patricia and Jesse left the dance. Patricia signed out of the dorm with her house mother, promising to make curfew. Curfew had been extended from midnight to 1:00 a.m. because of the occasion. Then Jesse and Patricia drove off from Watts to park on a secluded lovers' lane. They never returned.

The next day (Saturday), fellow students noticed Patricia missing and were concerned. She was considered responsible, and this was not like her. Hospitals were called and the police notified, but no investigation started. Her Watts Nursing School friends, knowing where they likely went, checked out cul-de-sacs until they found Jesse's car. It was parked in the developing Croasdaile residential area. Roads had been cut in but houses not built yet. The car was at the end of Wayside Place off Medford Road. Medford runs into Cole Mill Road, just a few miles from the Cabelands. The car was locked, undamaged and abandoned. Two coats lay across the back seat. Patricia's panty hose was neatly folded on the passenger floorboard. Everything appeared normal. Nothing was in disarray. There were no signs of a struggle.

Durham Police were contacted again and responded. They did determine the car was wiped clean of fingerprints. But their initial supposition was the couple may have eloped. It took a couple of days before everyone realized something was very wrong. For ten days, a frantic search was undertaken with both Durham and Orange County detectives working numerous leads, trying to find Patricia and Jesse. It was surveyor Robert Kirby who found them nearly two weeks after the dance.

Jesse and Patricia were tied to a large oak tree. Their hands were bound with thick ropes behind their backs. Other ropes were stretched tight and knotted around their necks. They had been strangled to death. Although still tied to the tree, their upper bodies had slumped over, lying side by side next to each other. There were little troughs scratched in the dirt where their feet had thrashed around. There were no signs of theft. Jesse was still wearing his class ring and watch. There were no signs of sexual assault. Their bodies appeared to have been pushed over and intentionally covered with leaves.

The medical examiner's autopsy revealed more. They discovered both Patricia and Jesse had multiple strangle marks on their necks, as though the rope had been tightened and loosened repeatedly. It was speculated they were tortured, choked to unconsciousness and allowed to revive, only to have the horror repeated. Patricia had a half-inch tear to her liver, which may have been caused by a punch to the stomach. Both had puncture wounds to the chest, but those were probably inflicted postmortem. Possibly the murderer was checking to see if they reacted so he or she would know they were dead.

The crime was investigated by the Durham County Sheriff's Office, Orange County Sheriff's Office and the North Carolina State Bureau of Investigation. The investigation went on for years, and three viable suspects were developed. Two of them had connections to each other. The case went cold but has been reopened several times. In 2018, the Orange County Sheriff's Office performed an intense reinvestigation of the case. At the time, one of the suspects was still living. There has never been enough evidence to make an arrest.

Patricia Mann is buried at Cool Springs Baptist Church in her hometown of Sanford. Her tombstone inscription highlights her career choice, "Service Beyond Self." Jesse McBane is buried at Mount Olive Baptist Church in Alamance County.

*There is much more to know about the Mann/McBane murders, enough to fill a whole book. If their story interests you, I highly recommend the podcast,* The Long Dance, *https://thelongdancepodcast.com. Sanzene Road was drivable in 1971. It can still be followed but now it has trees growing in it. In 1972, there was a similar case in nearby Duke Forest. A man with a pistol tried to force a couple into a car trunk, pistol-whipping the young man, but they managed to escape.*

# Mystery at Eno Beach

## Sunday–Tuesday, October 22–24, 1972

An early colonial road crossed the Eno at Fews Ford. Such a good crossing may have been an Indian path before William Few Sr. built his mill there in 1759. Nowadays, the ford is one of the most popular features in Eno River State Park. Children and dogs play there, hikers cross, rangers teach schoolchildren how water bugs reflect water quality. In the 1960s and '70s, before the state park, it was a different kind of place with a different kind of crowd. It was a hangout for drunken parties and motorcycle gangs. People washed their trucks in the ford, and trash abounded. Twenty years later, I would take my boys down to the ford, and we would amuse ourselves finding

Fews Ford, also known as Eno Beach.

bullet shells submerged among the rocks. During the '70s, the neighborhood called it Cates Ford for the family that owned it. People who came to party called it Eno Beach. In the events following October 22, 1972, news reports and court documents referred to it by both names. It wasn't until 1989, at the urging of the Eno River Association, that the state restored the oldest known historical name to the ford.

In October 1972, forty-one-year-old William T. Hollingsworth of Pulaski, Virginia, was doing time at the Durham County Correctional Unit. It was off Guess Road, adjacent to West Point on the Eno City Park, a quarter-mile uphill from the river, four and a half miles east of "Eno Beach." Hollingsworth had been there since March, serving three years for two counts of forcible trespass. The original charges were for forgery but had been pleaded down. In his opinion, ten months incarcerated were satisfactory, and on Sunday, October 22, just after dark, Hollingsworth scaled the fence and escaped.

In those days, the roads around Fews Ford were very different than we see today. They were narrow and plain dirt, taking a different track. Cole Mill Road was gravel, turning to dirt and dead ending at the ford. On Tuesday morning, not forty-eight hours from the escape, two men driving past the ford found a heavily tattooed body in the shallow water. Durham's escaped convict had been found. The body was in bad shape. Orange County sheriff C.D. Knight said in an interview, "It sure looks like he had an enemy, he was beaten up pretty badly." An attendant at the Chapel Hill Funeral Home told the *Durham Morning Herald*, "It looked like they used a hatchet on him, his head was in bad shape." A wound behind Hollingworth's ear led Sheriff Knight to believe the convict had been shot. However, the autopsy determined he had been beaten to death about the head and body with a blunt instrument and had been dead in the river less than twenty-four hours. He was found wearing his prison clothes: T-shirt, dark trousers, socks and shoes.

Officers from the sheriff's office and the North Carolina State Bureau of Investigation took on the case and made remarkable progress. On October 26, three days after the murder, they arrested Aubrey Donahue of Durham and charged him with planning and arranging Hollingsworth's escape and, according to the warrant, "procuring, counseling, and commanding" one Harold Lee Gilliam to murder Hollingsworth "in the Eno River at the end of Cole Mill Road in a place known as Eno Beach." The charge of murder was added to Donahue four days later.

The day after Donahue's arrest, Durham Police picked up Harold Gilliam at his home in Durham and turned him over to Orange County deputies, who charged him with murder. The same day, an arrest warrant for the murder was also issued for Henry Leon Hunsuckle, also of Durham. Hunsuckle went on the lam, hiding out until he was caught and arrested in January, two and a half months later. Then, just over a month after his arrest, on February 21, 1973, Hunsuckle pleaded guilty to prison escape and second-degree murder (original charge first-degree murder). His court-appointed attorney advised him not to plead, in order for his attorneys to have time to examine his case further. But Hunsuckle wanted to plead. He testified that he had helped Hollingworth escape, drove him around and then beat him fatally with a tire iron. He was sentenced to twenty-five years in prison. It looked like the mysteries of what transpired after Hollingsworth's prison break leading up to his death were being revealed. But then the story took a turn.

In fact, it took several turns. Both Donahue and Gilliam were scheduled to go to trial later in 1973. They did not plead guilty, and in October, the district attorney dismissed their charges with leave to reopen. This is typically done when the state doesn't have adequate evidence to proceed and plans to continue investigation. But the cases never reopened. Then in 1975, Hunsuckle appealed his conviction. He wrote a letter to the judge saying the only reason he pleaded guilty was out of fear of Harold

Gilliam. He claimed Gilliam threatened his life and that of his parents if he did not confess, and he knew Gilliam would carry out his threats. He went on the run after the murder because he knew Gilliam could force him to confess.

Hunsuckle was appointed an attorney, and his case went as far as the North Carolina Court of Appeals but was denied. The court determined Hunsuckle signed his confession and plea voluntarily and never told his attorney that he feared Gilliam. Hunsuckle was paroled in 1983 after serving more than ten years. And we are left with a lot of questions.

Because there was no trial for any of the defendants, there are no court transcripts of the how and why of this incident. Did Hunsuckle really murder Hollingsworth, or did he confess out of fear? Why did these three men break Hollingsworth out of prison? What did they do in the more than twenty-four hours between the Sunday night escape and the fatal beating? Was the plan all along to murder him? Did something happen on Eno Beach to provoke the attack? What was the relationship between three young guys from Durham, ages twenty-two to twenty-five, and a forty-one-year-old convict from Pulaski, Virginia? Was Donahue the mastermind, and if so, why did he want Hollingsworth dead? Why Eno Beach? Was this a place these guys frequented? If this had been a celebrity murder or prominent citizen, news coverage would have been intense and more questions answered. But sadly, the murder of an obscure inmate only garnered basic newspaper coverage. Thus, fifty years later, we are left with mystery on Eno Beach.

# Riverside Assassination

## *Friday, February 26, 1988*

At the northeast corner of the Guess Road Bridge and the Eno River is a brick house. The backyard meanders down to the riverbank, and the Mountains to Sea Trail passes by. For a good while, it has been the home and office of the Eno River Association. From there, staff and volunteers work diligently to preserve and protect the natural, historical and cultural resources of the Eno. Land is conserved, water quality advocated, the Eno River Festival is planned. The house has been a place of great joy and success. But in February 1988, it was a haven of dark forces.

The office of the Eno River Association and former home of Ineva Tapp.

In 1988, the house was the home of Ineva Tapp. On a Friday night, between seven and eight o' clock, Tapp's employee and close friend Betty Hudson Riley parked a car in the backyard. The house appeared deserted.

Forty-two-year-old Betty Riley was a Durham native. She lived not far away on Kirk Road. Betty was an administrative assistant at Neva's Rest Home on Cole Mill Road, which was owned by Ineva Tapp. It was Tapp's green four-door Plymouth that Riley was driving, something she did often. Whether she knew it or not, when she parked in that dark backyard, Betty was not alone. After she got out of the car, someone shot her in the face and left her dead, face down in the yard.

The residents came home at eight o'clock and found the car and Riley. Durham County Sheriff's Office was called. Responding deputies found the Plymouth's engine and lights off but keys still in the ignition. The family told the deputies that no one expected Riley that evening. The woods of West Point on the Eno Park are behind the backyard, and deputies searched those woods late into the night seeking evidence.

Betty Riley was laid to rest in a graveside service on Monday, February 29, at the Markham Memorial Garden in Durham. Before the funeral, family and friends gathered at the home of Ineva Tapp's daughter Brenda Riley.

Remember that name as this tale unfolds. Brenda was not a blood relative of Betty but lived next door on Kirk Road.

The same day as the funeral, sheriff's investigators announced they were looking for a certain man for questioning regarding the slaying. A composite sketch was released to the newspapers. Detective R.D. Buchanan was leading the investigation. He said they were seeking a man who acted suspicious at Batten Quick Stop Friday night. The store was less than half a mile north on Guess Road from Tapp's house. Witnesses said the man appeared nervous and told the clerk to hurry up and give him the change from the ten-dollar bill with which he paid for his soda. The man looked out the front window of the store and said he had to go somewhere or meet someone. He was described as five feet, ten inches to six feet tall, 180 to 185 pounds, with a mustache, short hair and medium smooth complexion.

Ten days after the murder, the intrigue grew. Ineva Tapp, in whose backyard the murder took place, was revealed as one of four people a local elderly couple had plotted to have murdered. Crawford James Blake, seventy-two, and his wife Valley Walker Blake, sixty-five, pleaded guilty in Durham Court to charges of solicitation to commit murder. The Blakes lived at Caroline Trailer Park, next to Eno River State Park's Cabelands Access. In June 1987, the Blakes offered $5,000 to a member of the Ku Klux Klan (KKK) to kill four people they believed were involved in the unsolved murders of their two sons. One son, Crawford Blake Jr., was murdered in 1985 in his home on Dumont Drive, which coincidentally has a neighborhood access into the state park. The other son, Larry Riley, was murdered in 1981 in Harnett County and left in a ditch. The four people slated for the revenge also included Brenda Riley, the same Brenda whose house family had gathered in before Betty's funeral. But wait! There's more! The murdered victim, Betty Riley, was the first wife of the murdered son Larry Riley. His second wife? Betty's next-door neighbor, Brenda.

To move the murder-for-hire plot forward, the Blakes also provided their KKK contact a shotgun. The Blakes solicited this contact after seeing his participation in a KKK rally. What tripped up the plot was the person the Blakes solicited was actually an undercover North Carolina State Bureau of Investigation agent. With all this to consider, Detective Buchanan didn't know whether Betty Riley's murder by the Eno was intentional or a case of mistaken identity. Was it a result of the Blake's plan of vengeance?

By mid-March, Durham Crimestoppers was offering $1,200 for information leading to an arrest in Betty Riley's murder. Their posting noted a motive had not been determined. The case went cold. In July 1992,

Raleigh's *News and Observer* reported the Durham sheriff had a suspect and thought it was a contract killing. However, no record exits in the press or the Durham Courthouse of any subsequent arrest in the murder, leaving Betty Riley wanting for justice.

# Curious Clothing Caper at Cabelands

## *Wednesday, June 2, 1993*

It's usually great to be a ranger on the Eno, but the summer of 1993 was tough. We had only two rangers in the whole state park. There had been a lot of car break-ins at Cabelands parking lot, which aggravated us because we really care about the visitor experience. Most of the parking was for the Eno Quarry, which while not yet part of the state park was the easiest starting point to walk from. Even though we had a lot of park to cover, Ranger Scott Hartley and I would schedule times individually to do Cabelands parking lot surveillance.

We would watch from the woods with binoculars, sitting in a chair. We couldn't really hide because then we couldn't get a good view of the cars. Our only camouflage was our green and gray uniforms. It didn't matter. This was when I learned people are so focused on themselves that they are oblivious to what is going on around them. No one ever saw us. One time I was sitting twenty-five yards back in the woods and a car pulled into a space directly facing me. A passenger jumped out, ran into the woods right at me, stopped five yards from me, relieved himself, went back to the car and never saw me.

The evening of June 2, I parked my patrol car along the park boundary at Caroline Trailer Park on Howe Street. I walked up through the woods and set up my chair to sit and watch the parking lot. At almost seven o'clock, groups of teens were returning to their cars in waves. Brian Barton, who I was to meet shortly, was in the second group. He went to a white-and-green pickup truck and lifted the hard-shell bed cover. From the bed he started distributing new clothes to the other kids. These were clothes on hangers, with price tags, brand labels and security tags. There were about ten teenagers going through the clothes and taking some as they left. I was wondering if I had stumbled on a fly-by-night flea market. Doubting I could get control of a group this size, I waited until the herd thinned.

Eventually it got down to Barton and three others, trying on clothes and looking at their reflections in the truck mirrors. Barton got into his truck and changed into new shorts. He threw the tag on the ground and tossed the security tag in the woods. After watching this puzzling activity for twenty minutes, I slipped back up to my Chevy Blazer and drove around to the parking lot. Barton looked at me as I got out and shoved the clothes on the tailgate back into the truck bed, shutting the tailgate and bed cover.

I got to questioning the four remaining, asking whether clothes were being sold, which is not permitted in a state park. I was assured no sales were going on, and I asked where the clothes came from. Barton said he worked for Rock Art in Chapel Hill and was delivering the clothes from one store to another. Naturally, I asked why other kids were taking clothes away. His answer was they were also delivering the clothes since they could get to the store earlier than he could and the clothes needed to be there by 9:00 p.m. I was going from a little suspicious to full intrigue, told him so, and asked a lot more questions. These questions included whether he had any weapons or drugs. Eventually, I asked if I could search his truck, to which Barton readily agreed.

Lots of clothes were lying in the truck bed along with two duffle bags also stuffed with clothes. There was a hip pack. I asked who owned the pack, and no one claimed it. Barton told me a lot of people ride in his truck and anyone could have left it. He said to go ahead and look in it. Inside were two multicolored ceramic smoking pipes with wire screens and residue smelling of marijuana. In legal terms, this is drug paraphernalia.

With the complexity of the situation growing, I realized that backup would be useful. I attempted to radio the Orange County Sheriff's Office, but radio communications between the county and the park back then were clumsy to ineffective. However, my wife, listening on the scanner at home, heard me and telephoned the 911 center. Communication settled and help on the way, with permission I continued the search of everyone and their stuff.

It was almost 8:00 p.m. when Deputy David Hughes arrived. We both questioned the boys individually but got nothing on where the clothes came from or why they were being handed out. Deputy Hughes radioed for someone to go by Rock Art and check, but no one was available and the phone number in the book (we had phonebooks in those days) was not current. We knew something untoward was up and didn't want to lose Barton, so we came to the consensus to arrest him for drug paraphernalia. Because Barton was just nineteen years old, cooperative and worried about his truck, we let him drive to the magistrate following Deputy

Hughes with me tailing. The magistrate put him under a $500 unsecured bond and released him.

I did try to call Rock Art the next day, having found a valid phone number, but it wasn't until two days after the parking lot incident that I got ahold of someone at their store. Their immediate response was to ask me to hang on because the police had just arrived to investigate their stolen clothes. The store manager handed the phone to a Chapel Hill police officer. It turns out that Brian Barton was a former employee of Rock Art. The clothing had been stored in a van parked outside the store, and they didn't know it was missing until that morning. Lucky for them, I had all the information they needed to find their culprit. Brian Barton was subsequently convicted of the larceny. I do remember him being quite cheerful in the parking lot when we first arrested him and again when his case came to court.

# Into Our Waiting Arms

## Sunday, July 7, 1996

A guest of the North Carolina Department of Corrections (DOC) was ready to go home. Twenty-seven-year-old Jay Castleberry of Lee County was on an extended stay at their facility on the hill above the Eno River's south bank, a short distance off Guess Road in Durham. Castleberry found himself in these circumstances due to a propensity for breaking and entering. Now he was ready to terminate his unfortunate incarceration. He had a plan, and he had help. Knowing staffing would be low on the July Fourth holiday weekend, he would make his move, escaping and following the river to West Point at the Eno City Park, where his girlfriend would pick him up in her car.

In the morning, when no one was looking, he threw a mattress over the barbed wire and climbed the fence, dropping to freedom. From there he quickly ran into the woods and scrambled down the steep slope to the river where he turned right, downriver toward West Point. He was a mile from being in his sweet baby's car.

Castleberry must have lived under a rock, because everyone knows the biggest Independence Day festival in North Carolina happens every July Fourth weekend at West Point on the Eno. The annual Festival for the Eno is one of the safest places in the state, as every year the Durham Sheriff's Office

The riverbank downhill from the old Durham prison.

provides a large contingent of officers to monitor on-site. As our unhappy guest was picking his way through the brush, prison guards discovered his unauthorized absence and released the hounds—bloodhounds, that is. Actually, they didn't release them but set them on the trail on long leads. It was Durham police dog Bern followed by his handler Officer Moses Irving who had no trouble deducing their rabbit had run to the river and was heading for West Point. If you know that side of the river, it is steep and treacherous, so Bern and Irving turned back. But with a direction of travel determined, the call came over every deputy's radio at the festival.

Meanwhile, things weren't going well for the girlfriend. She also didn't know about the Eno River Festival, nor were private vehicles allowed in the park during the festival. To go to the festival, you park at the Durham County Stadium and take a two-mile bus ride into the park. When she got to the park, she was turned away by the ranger at the gate.

Greg Bell was on festival staff that year. He would go on to become the longest-tenured Festival for the Eno director. What he remembers from that day was the wave of deputies running down the hill to the river. The deputies split into two groups and crouched in the bushes on both sides of the river, watching upstream. Our clueless escapee was congratulating himself as he walked the shoreline, up until Sheriff's Lieutenant C.R. Vaughn stood up abruptly in front of him, backed up by a herd of deputies. Two hours after the escapade began, it came to an anticlimactic end. Immediately handcuffed and marched to a patrol car, he confessed the whole plan and even ratted out his girlfriend, who was subsequently arrested.

*The Guess Road prison unit closed in 2011, so we don't expect to encounter more inmates taking unauthorized hikes on the Eno.*

# Darkness Falls on Cabelands

## *Friday, October 3, 1997*

The Cabelands Access of Eno River State Park is the trailhead for the sparkling Cabe Gorge and the Eno Quarry and the first lands donated to create the park. The stone walls of the Cabe Mill and tombstones of a family cemetery are tucked out of sight in the woods. In October 1997, the Cabelands parking lot off Howe Street was ungated. Most of the state park accesses on the river had gates that were locked at night, but there were unsecured areas where you could get into the park after hours, whether you were supposed to or not. If rangers got all the gates shut before the end of their shift, they would often check these access points for late-night illicit activity.

We had been reluctant to put a gate up at Cabelands because driving around to open and close another gate is one more task on a small staff already stretched in its responsibilities. But over the summer and into the fall of 1997, we were finding more and more evidence of after-hours activity at Cabelands usually in the form of trash or vandalism. There is also a regulation that a permit is required to be on a state park at night (usually a camping permit), and it's not fair to people who have paid for night access to have other folks coming out and using the park for free. At our September staff meeting, rangers and maintenance came to a consensus: we needed a gate at the Cabelands. Planning started, but on October 3, the gate was not up yet.

It was a Friday night, and Ranger Greg Schneider was on the closing shift. As his supervisor, I can testify that Ranger Schneider had an uncanny ability to discern when trouble was afoot and slink up on problem people without

Cabelands Access parking lot, Eno River State Park.

being noticed. After getting the rest of the park put to bed, he drove over to Cabelands to check the parking lot. On this night, he decided to drive past the parking lot, park his patrol vehicle in the adjacent trailer park and watch for a few minutes. The parking lot is dark but illuminated by a streetlight at the entrance. It didn't take long before a car drove into the lot. Behind the wheel was Doug Hilliard.

Exiting his truck, Schneider walked carefully through the woods to the parking lot, coming up behind the running car. He stood behind a pine tree, about twenty feet from the car, and watched. Hilliard was sitting in the driver's seat, drinking from a can. He finished and threw the can out the window. Schneider immediately started for the car. At a minimum it was littering, which never sits well with park rangers, and it may have been a drunk driving situation. But as Schneider was exiting the woods, Hilliard put the car in gear and began driving out of the parking lot. Schneider ran in front of the car, identified himself and yelled for the Hilliard to stop the car. But the car didn't stop, at least until it bumped into the ranger, fortunately at slow speed, pushing him back a foot or two.

Schneider ordered the driver to turn off the motor and get out of the car. Hilliard did as he was told and came out saying he didn't know he wasn't supposed to be down here and he just came to meet a girl! Schneider asked him what he threw out of the car and Hilliard told him it was a Pepsi can. It was no great surprise, but the Pepsi can had morphed into a Budweiser beer can before it hit the ground. Hilliard offered to pick it up, but Schneider told him he would take care of it and asked Hilliard for his driver's license. Hilliard said he left it at home, but the truth was it was permanently revoked. He did tell Schneider his name, address and date of birth, which Schneider recorded in his field notebook. This is when things started to get complicated.

This was a time before the park had direct radio communications with Orange County for law enforcement purposes. Our agreement with the county allowed for them to provide law enforcement information to us only by telephone, but this was also before cellphones were common and Schneider did not have one. We did have radio communications over the county fire channel, and he did request the dispatcher confirm the identification and check for warrants, but rightfully so, the dispatcher could not provide the information on that channel. Schneider repeatedly tried to radio off-duty rangers to make the phone call, but because of the late hour, it was hard to find one. Finally, an off-duty ranger at Falls Lake listening on a scanner responded and made the call.

Meanwhile, Ranger Schneider told Hilliard he would be cited for littering, and a conversation ensued. Hilliard said again he would go get the can and made a crude statement explaining his presence in the parking lot. Schneider told Hilliard he was watching the lot because there had been a lot of drug use there. Hilliard said he did not use drugs, which of course was his next lie. A blood test later that night would be positive for cocaine. Hilliard even offered to let Schneider look in the car for drugs. As Schneider began writing the littering ticket, Hilliard asked if he could smoke. Schneider first told him no, but Hilliard was persistent, so he relented and told him he could only if he stood well away where Schneider wouldn't have to breathe the smoke.

While Schneider was writing the ticket, a cellphone rang in the car and Hilliard ducked in inside and got it before Schneider could stop him. Still, he allowed Hilliard to finish his call and then asked for the phone number for the citation. Hilliard said he didn't have a phone. Schneider asked him about the cellphone he was just using. Hilliard said it wasn't his, it belonged to the business he worked for. Schneider asked who he worked for. Hilliard said he was a self-employed painter. He finally, grudgingly, gave Schneider the phone number. Schneider finished up the ticket.

About this time, the Falls Lake ranger radioed back with all kinds of information. This is when Schneider learned of the driver's license revocation. Hilliard's address on his state issued ID card didn't match the address he gave. He had expired warrants for domestic violence. And the license plate on the car belonged to another car! Hilliard had excuses for everything and said the car belonged to his sister.

After Schneider handed Hilliard the ticket, he told Hilliard he could not drive the car out of there and offered to drive him to a convenience store where he could call for a ride, or Hilliard could walk from the Cabelands. Then, even though Hilliard had previously made the offer, Schneider asked him, "Since you don't do drugs, you won't mind me looking in the car"? Hilliard replied, "No sir, go ahead," and opened the driver's door. Normal procedure when a ranger searches a car is to have the driver wait in a location safe for the ranger and the driver. Schneider told Hilliard to stand in front of the car, but Hilliard kept coming back to the door to watch the search. Right off the bat, Schneider found rolling papers under the armrest and a little bag of cocaine in the ashtray. With that, Schneider told Hilliard to put his hands on the hood. Hilliard did start to comply but then took off running into the dark trailer park. Hilliard would later testify in court that he sized up the ranger and thought he could outrun him. As circumstances would play out, they were pretty evenly matched. Schneider ran after Hilliard, ordering him to stop. While running, he managed to radio the Falls Lake ranger and requested backup from the Orange County Sheriff's Department. As he ran, he lost his ball cap and thought he lost his notebook. Remember this for later.

Hilliard ran a circle between the trailers and headed back to his car. Schneider yelled after him, ordering him to stay away from the car. Ignoring the ranger, Hilliard got in and shut the door. Slowing to a walk, under the lit parking lot entrance, Schneider yelled, "Don't start the car." He drew his gun, aiming at the car. Hilliard started the car. Schneider yelled, "If you try to hit me, I will shoot you," while walking forward to block the exit. Hilliard came at him with the car. Schneider yelled, "Stop or I will shoot," just before the car struck him in the legs, knocking him up on the hood! As he landed on the hood, Schneider grabbed the only thing he could with his left hand, the edge where the hood meets the windshield. His revolver was still in his right hand. Hilliard drove out of the parking lot, turned left onto Howe Street and accelerated. Schneider yelled repeatedly, "Stop the car," but Hilliard just sped up. Schneider aimed his gun through the windshield and fired twice, hitting Hilliard both times. The two holes in the windshield were three and a half inches apart.

Hilliard slammed on the brakes, and Schneider rolled off the hood, landing in front of the left tire. Hilliard looked out the window and said, "You SOB, you shot me!" Schneider later recalled, "I saw the left wheel turning toward me and could hear the car's power steering pump grind as the wheels turned as far left as they could go." To escape being struck again, Schneider rolled into the ditch and then scrambled on all fours up into the woods. The car started in his direction and then straightened out and drove away on Howe Street. Schneider ran back to the parking lot radioing for assistance.

I was at a Red Cross banquet in Hillsborough where my wife was being honored for blood donation. Our fourteen-year-old babysitter paged me, and when I called her back, she told me "my friend" shot someone. I knew who was on duty and where he had planned to patrol so I didn't need any clarification. Within an hour of Schneider first arriving at the Cabelands, the Orange County Sheriff's Office and multiple state park rangers, including myself, were on scene. The first ranger to arrive was the Falls Lake superintendent. I didn't want to know how fast he drove. The State Bureau of Investigation (SBI) rolled in soon after. We were up all night with the investigation.

Meanwhile, Hilliard drove to a trailer park on Highway 70 between Hillsborough and Durham, where a resident called for an ambulance. It didn't take long for the sheriff's department to connect the two scenes. EMTs took Hilliard to Duke Hospital. Deputies and rangers secured his car, and two rangers sat with it all night until it could be towed to fenced storage at Falls Lake to be secured as evidence. Remember the lost notebook? Orange County sheriff Lindy Pendergrass found it stuffed between the hood and windshield.

Six days later, as Hilliard was discharged from Duke, two Falls Lake rangers and I arrested him at the hospital on eight charges and drove him to the Orange County Jail. As we waited for the magistrate, he asked me to tell Schneider that he was sorry for what he had done and knew an apology would not change things. We let him use the bathroom and at his request let him smoke. Smoking was big mistake, as within minutes, combined with his injuries, it nearly shut down his breathing. I helped him to the ground and five paramedics responded, giving him oxygen. He recovered and, after going in front of the magistrate, was immediately bailed out by family.

At the time of his arrest, Hilliard had thirty-five criminal convictions, eight traffic convictions, fourteen charges dismissed and fourteen pending cases, including ours. In his statements to the SBI, Hilliard told them he did not use drugs (they knew otherwise from the blood test) and that he had four or five beers in the three hours before getting to the state park. He also claimed that Schneider "jumped" onto the hood of the car. He went to trial in April 1998 at the Hillsborough Courthouse. Hilliard was convicted, with the two main charges being assault with a deadly weapon with intent to kill a law enforcement officer and possession of cocaine. He ended up doing several months of prison time for the cocaine charge; however, the judge said being shot was enough punishment for the assault. With a touch of irony, Hilliard ended up on a prison work crew down east doing work at a state park.

# Occoneechee Mountain Murder

## *Thursday, September 28, 2000*

On what seemed like a normal Thursday morning, I was getting into my patrol car for a day of work on the Eno River State Park. I heard Bob Cook (no relation) call Wayne Watson on the radio. Cook was a maintenance worker and Watson our maintenance chief. I knew Cook should be doing the opening routine at Occoneechee Mountain. Cook told Watson he needed to come to Occoneechee now. His tone told me something was very wrong, and I needed to get there and get there fast. Without knowing why, I hauled it from Fews Ford.

In those days, the park gate for Occoneechee Mountain was not out by Orange Grove Road like it is now. Virginia Cates Road, the entrance road into Occoneechee, parallels Interstate 85 for 350 yards with a steep wooded hillside in between. Then the road curves into the park interior. The gate had to be set back in that curve because the parallel stretch is in the I-85 right-of-way and the North Carolina Department of Transportation did not want to turn over control of the road to state parks. That might interfere with their plans to widen the interstate, which twenty-four years later has not started. It took intercession from the Eno River Association to the Board of Transportation to get the road under state park control. We were still a couple of years from that happening on this day. Meanwhile, we frequently found leftover evidence of illicit after-hours activity at the gate. It was a dark, secluded place at night.

I got to the park entrance fast to find Bob standing by Hillsborough resident Albert Carr, who was lying in the road a short distance in front of

The road to Occoneechee Mountain. The old gate was in the far curve.

the gate, a beer can tucked in his arm, his soul departed. He appeared to have a gunshot wound. I called in the Orange County Sheriff's Office and then called my supervisor, North District superintendent Susan Tillotson. Carr was dead on the state park boundary. I asked Tillotson whether we should take the lead on the investigation, which would mean calling in the State Bureau of Investigation, or should lead be give it to the sheriff's office. She asked how much of him was in the park. I answered truthfully that it looked like an arm and leg were in the park and the rest outside. She said give it to the sheriff.

I quickly surmised the deputies responding had no love for Carr. He had been arrested just the day before in a drug raid. They knew him well for his criminal activity and for what had happened in the town of Roanoke Rapids. Carr had done time for killing Roanoke Rapids police officer Sonny Vaughn when Carr was nineteen years old. Officer Vaughn was shot four times in the chest during a gunfight at a convenience store robbery. Carr was sentenced to life in 1977. He did ten years.

I can assure you that during this and all other cooperative investigations with the Orange County Sheriff's Office there was the utmost professionalism. However, this time there was some unexpected laughter. When I asked the deputies what was so amusing, they pointed out Carr was lying feet away from an "Alcoholic Beverages Prohibited" sign with that beer can tucked in his arm. They told me, "You rangers take that alcohol stuff serious!"

As investigation ensued, a deputy and I went out near Orange Grove Road to control public and media access. While watching the scene from afar, we saw a wave of deputies suddenly run up the hill to the interstate. It turns out there was a second victim. Robert Clegg, a wanted man by the state Department of Corrections, was on the interstate shoulder, shot in the leg. He had fled from his assailants and hid in brush along the interstate. About 10:00 a.m., he eased out of hiding and was seen crawling beside the highway. Now we had a live witness.

Sheriff's investigators were able to determine the incident was a drug deal gone bad. Clegg named two suspects. They were bad company and in the drug trade. There never was a conviction though. Clegg left town, so there was no witness and not enough evidence to convict. Despite this incident, it still took years for DOT to give us permission to put a gate where it would effectively keep the drug trade out.

# Old Farm Killing

## Tuesday, February 17, 2004

The first indication there was trouble on the Eno came starkly and four days late. On Saturday, February 21, 2004, a group of teenage boys from the Durham-Chapel Hill Strikers were preparing for the season's first soccer game at Old Farm Park. Old Farm Park is on the south bank and in a sharp bend of the river in north Durham. The park has ball fields, picnic tables and children's swings. It is surrounded by a nice residential neighborhood. Most of the park is open field and mowed, but there is a thin strip of woods along the river. The park attracts families and sports teams during the day, but neighbors say it can be a seedy scene of illicit activity at night.

Four or five soccer players were exploring around in the woods near the river when they spotted the body of a man floating face down in the water. The body was shirtless and wearing blue jeans. At 12:42 p.m., a parent called Durham Police. More than a dozen police, fire and swift water rescue responded. They hoisted the body up a fifteen-foot embankment to the

Durham's Old Farm Park.

sound of soccer cleats pummeling a ball fifty yards away. It was Seth Ethan Owen, twenty-three years old, of Franklinton, North Carolina.

Owen was born Michael Owens Jr., but he changed his name when his identity was stolen. He was a churchgoer. He called his parents and grandparents every couple of days, but it was not unusual for him to be away from home. He was on probation in Franklin County for obtaining property with false pretenses. His family had no idea why he would be in Durham, as Owen had no friends there. He was last seen by his family on Tuesday, February 17, when he told his mother he was going to Raleigh to meet a friend named Blue whom he met on the internet. Earlier, he mentioned Blue to his sister Tiffany and showed her the cellphone he was using to text Blue. He said he intended to bring Blue back home with him. When Owen didn't come home after three days, his mother reported him missing.

At the time Owen's body was recovered, how he died and how long he had been in the river was a mystery. An autopsy was ordered, and they had one of the answers in a single day. Owen had been shot twice in the head.

From the beginning, the police were looking for Owen's burgundy Ford Contour. That car was his pride and joy, and he took exquisite care of it. The day after the body's discovery, police and firefighters found the car three blocks from the Durham Police Station, where someone had tried to set it on fire. Witnesses saw it parked about 7:30 a.m., and three people got out. The driver was reported to be Derrick Lamont Shuler of Chapel Hill. Shuler was wanted in connection for three armed robberies in Chapel Hill over the last three months. Shuler became an early suspect in Owen's death but was subsequently ruled out. Witnesses also told police the car was seen driving around the same neighborhood for the last three days. Police found the car unlocked, and a small fire had been started on the driver's seat.

Eleven days later, on Thursday, March 4, it was announced three men had been arrested for Owen's murder. They were Matthew Taylor, nicknamed Blue, a sixteen-year-old Northern High School student and football player; Shelton Epps, twenty-one; and Derrick Maiden, eighteen and a sophomore at Northern High School. Taylor and Epps lived together on Lazyriver Drive, directly across the Eno River from Old Farm Park. Maiden lived on Hummingbird Lane, a side street of Lazyriver. All three were held initially without bail in the Durham County Jail.

It did not take long for details of the crime to start coming out. Owen was killed at Old Farm Park on February 17, the same day he said good-bye to his mother. On February 18, his Ford Contour was parked behind Northern High School without a permit. A boot was put on it, and Taylor gave another student twenty-five dollars to get the boot removed, with instructions to deliver the car to Taylor. This same student said Taylor bragged about buying a gun in October and wanting to test it out. Police now believed robbery was the motive and Owen was lured to Durham through an internet chat line.

The day after the arrests, police executed a search warrant on Taylor's house, seizing .32-caliber shell casings, cellphones and drug paraphernalia. The house is within walking distance of where Owen was found in the river. From the cellphones they learned Owen and Taylor had been texting since the day before Owen disappeared, and a text message indicated they planned to meet in Durham on the day he died.

It was at an April bail hearing that the whole story came out. Taylor and Maiden weren't talking. But Epps had a tale to tell.

On February 17, Northern High School let out early for snow. The three conspirators gathered in the Lazyriver Drive house of Epps and Taylor. Epps and Maiden were playing video games. Taylor told them a tale of how someone else had used a chat line to steal a car, and he wanted to try it. So, Taylor used his cellphone to call Owen and arranged a meeting at their house, then grabbed his old .32-caliber revolver loaded with two bullets. In text messages, Taylor specifically asked Owen what kind of car he would be driving.

Despite the snow, Owen and his Ford Contour made it to the Lazyriver Drive house. Before even leaving the porch, Taylor told Epps and Maiden, if this guy wasn't smooth, he would shoot him. The three men asked Owen for a ride, and he took them to a store at the corner of Roxboro and Infinity Roads, up the hill from the Eno. Epps bought a cigar with the intent to use it to smoke marijuana. They surmised getting Owen high would facilitate the car theft. Driving south on Roxboro Road, they crossed over the river and turned left on Rippling Stream Road and drove to Old Farm Park. Getting out, Epps broke up the cigar and brought out the marijuana. This is when things escalated fast. Standing in front of the car, Taylor drew, cocked, and put the revolver to Owen's head.

Owen pleaded for his life, "Please don't do this to me," then turned and ran. Taylor fired, hitting Owen in the head. But Owen didn't go down or stop. The three assassins ran after him and caught him. Taylor and Epps wrestled him to the ground and all three hit him in the face. Owen got up and tried to get to the car so he could get inside, but they pulled him back. Somehow Epps got hold of the gun and tried to get a clean shot, but Owen kept fighting. Taylor, in frustration, took the gun back and shot Owen in the head again, but Owen wouldn't die and the attack continued.

Epps kicked Owen in the head once and stomped on it twice, while Maiden kicked him in the side. At some point, one of them tried to choke him. As Epps told it, he didn't understand why Taylor didn't just shoot Owen again, not knowing there were only two bullets. Taylor kept pulling the trigger on the empty gun. Owen was so hard to kill that Epps was thinking, "This boy is a soldier!" At this point, Owen was dead or nearly so. The threesome dragged him to the edge of the river and rolled him in. According to Epps, "We all said, 'We just did murder. We need to get out of here!'"

They took Owen's car and drove around, stopping so Epps could wipe blood off his hands in the snow. They bought another cigar and smoked marijuana. They removed a pair of Owen's boots from the trunk. Maiden was wearing those boots when the police first interviewed him.

In the aftermath, Epps burned his clothes. Taylor drove the stolen car to Northern High School, where it was subsequently booted. Five days later, after Owen's body had been found, Maiden, Epps and Taylor drove the car to Maiden Street in Durham. They wiped it down with bleach and doused the interior with lighter fluid. Epps used his lighter to start the unsuccessful fire.

The three murderers were indicted by a grand jury for murder, kidnapping and robbery. Prosecutor Freda Black said all three gave statements to the police and all three conflicted. Only Epps's statement from the bond hearing was made public. Taylor's trial began on July 11, 2005, fifteen months after the killing. Taylor's attorney argued that his client was present but did not participate, did not know the plan and was under the influence of the older men. But it was hard to explain away the text messages that lured Owen to the Eno in the first place. Even though Maiden was silent way back at the bond hearing, he testified against Taylor as part of a plea agreement. The trial lasted eight days. With three hours of deliberation, seventeen-year-old Taylor was found guilty of murder, kidnapping and robbery. He received a life sentence, plus six years.

Epps went on trial in February 2006, nearly two years after Owen's death. His attorney claimed Epps wasn't even in the park and his statement at the bond hearing was just telling police what they wanted to hear. The prosecutor pointed out Epps knew specific details of the crime only a participant would know. Maiden also testified against Epps. After a six-day trial and two-hour jury deliberation, Epps was found guilty of the same charges as Taylor and sentenced to life without parole.

Maiden was sentenced the day after Epps's conviction. He pleaded guilty to second-degree murder under the terms of his plea agreement in exchange for his testimony. Through tears, he apologized to his family, the court and Owen's family. Maiden was sentenced to a minimum of nine years and two months in state prison.

It was at Taylor's trial that the prosecution revealed a disturbing surprise about Owen's final moments. They announced that Owen was alive when rolled into the Eno. Cause of death was drowning.

## 3

# PHANTOMS

## The Ghost of Cole Mill

### *Thursday, December 16, 1880*

The Laurel Bluffs Trail from Guess Road to Pleasant Green Road is beautiful, passing the sparkling Eno River in high places through mountain laurel and shaded forest and along the expansive Eno Quarry. Take a day hike upriver, and about three hundred yards after passing under the Cole Mill Road Bridge, you may spot the grinding stones and earthen banks of the head and tailraces from the old Cole Mill. Take a night hike here in this place, and you may see something else entirely.

The mill operated from at least 1813 until the great flood of 1908 took it out. Like other mills on the river, its functions changed during the course of history. At times it was either a grist, tilt hammer or sawmill, probably based on what was profitable at the time. One thing was constant: a dam on the river diverted water into the headrace, a large ditch with raised earth banks. From there the diverted water flowed across the water wheel at the mill, giving power to gears and belts that drove the grinding stones, saw blade or tilt hammer. For the mill's final forty-two years, John Anderson Cole oversaw its operation. He had five sons working for him. Their home place was one hundred yards up the hill from the mill.

There are times when you wish you could take back the last five seconds of your life and make a different choice.

In December 1880, Cole Mill was sawing lumber. On this day, a couple of the Cole boys were working. Twenty-six-year-old Wiley DeWitt "Dee" Cole made a fatal tragic mistake he wished he could take back. Dee Cole put his knee down on the sawmill belt. The belt gripped the fabric of his trousers and ripped him into the saw blade. Instantly, his right arm was sliced off. It fell in the millrace and washed away. As he was trying to pull himself free from the grip of the spinning blade, Dee's kneecap was cut off. His brother tried to help. He carried Dee from the mill, but as they struggled up the hill to the house, the brother fainted and injured Dee had to catch him.

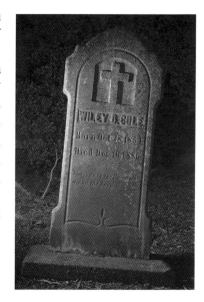

They made it to the house. This was before cars and telephones, so there was only one way to get help. A friend jumped on a horse and rode as fast as he could to get the nearest doctor, on Roxboro Road, more than five miles away. When he got there, the doctor was out, so there was even more delay before medical attention reached Dee. The stories conflict as to which of Drs. Battle, Cain, or Smith responded. It may have been any combination of all three. What is known is in an effort to save Dee's life, they amputated what remained of his right arm and his leg above where the saw severed. The bleeding before and after surgery was profuse. Blood soaked through the mattress on to the wooden floor. It is said the bloodstains never came out of the floor. About eight o'clock that evening, Wiley DeWitt Cole breathed his last—cause of death was blood loss.

The elderly Jesse Cole was interviewed in 1986. She had lived in the house until age twelve and was told that Dee was put in a casket in the big room of the house and blood ran through the casket, staining the floor permanently. Could be the story got changed over time. Dee was buried at Pleasant Green Church. His tombstone is there, close to his parents.

It was soon after the funeral that the happenings began. People started reporting strange lights and noises at night down by the river. Some people reported seeing a ghost walking the millrace, holding his head

*Above*: Feral millstone on the site of the old Cole Mill.

*Opposite*: Wiley DeWitt Cole is buried at Pleasant Green Methodist Church.

under his arm. One evening when Jesse Cole was just a little girl, she was in the kitchen while her mama was in there grinding coffee. The tenant who lived in a small house on the property came by with a strange look on his face and a tale. He said he had just seen a man walking up the river. The man was perfect except he didn't have a head! Jesse never forgot Mama's response. Mama said, "That's just Dee!" There was never an explanation of how a man that lost his leg and arm was headless, but people saw what they saw. However, Mama never let the kids play at the river alone.

The state park is closed at night, so you can't really hike the Laurel Bluffs Trail in the dark. But you may spend the night at the Piper Creek Campground a mile upriver. Maybe Dee Cole will visit you there.

*In the 1960s and '70s, the Eno River Association made a concentrated effort to collect oral histories in their campaign to save the Eno River from being dammed. Thanks to this project we have the story of "The Ghost of Cole Mill," which came to us from three sources. It first appeared in the 1980 Eno River Calendar. To see a video presentation of this story on location visit: https://www.youtube.com/watch?v=IlxAvPQtlGk.*

# The Hillsborough Beast

## February–March 1903

Hillsborough was quintessential small-town North Carolina—quiet, pretty and surrounded by tranquil farmland. But in the late winter of 1903, the town residents were in a stir. Great excitement prevailed. Coming at night, a mysterious wild animal was attacking cattle and dogs.

Even though the town was surrounded by rural countryside, dangerous wild animals were eradicated decades before. No one could remember seeing a bear or cougar since the days of youth of the oldest people in Hillsborough. Townsfolk were afraid to go out on the streets at night. If they had to go out, they carried a lantern and a musket. At first daylight, everyone would go into their yards and barn lots, fearful of finding their pet dog or their cattle suffering from a midnight massacre.

Rumors were permeating as to what kind of terrifying beast had taken up residence. Some said it was a wildcat (bobcat), like a thirty-pound cat taking down a cow was realistic! Others suggested it was a panther, and one local lawyer said he saw it in his yard and it looked like a panther to him. Perhaps it was a lion or tiger escaped from a circus or a private collector. It was even suggested it was the Hound of the Baskervilles and Sherlock Holmes didn't actually kill it dead. One thing was for sure: whatever it was, it was leaving a lot of tracks in the soft soil on the edge of the Eno River. These tracks were frequently seen, but no one in town had the knowledge to recognize whose tracks they were.

The attacks went on for several weeks, but by mid-March, they had ceased. Hillsborough went back to peaceful nights. The identity of the wild beast disappeared in town lore.

# Little Girl Ghost

## 1966

Near the intersection of the Buckquarter Creek and Ridge Trails in Eno River State Park is the crumbling, two-story log home known as the Anthony Cole house. In the winter, with leaves off the trees, you can see the house from the trails. The marks of an axe can still be seen in the hewn logs.

Look up to the underside of the tin roof, and original wood shakes that once shingled the roof are visible. Anthony never lived there. He had it built for his son Thomas around 1850. The last occupant was Grover Cleveland Shaw, who used the house as a personal retreat until he sold his land to Eno River State Park in 1977. Even when Shaw was staying there, the house was deteriorating. The kitchen in the back collapsed before I ever saw it, and I have watched the house sag more and more for thirty years. Since the state park took over, the only inhabitants are the black vultures nesting in the attic—or are they?

In 1966, descendant Mark Cole Jr. came out to see the birthplace of his father. His father was born in the house ninety years earlier in 1876 but lived there only a few years before moving to Cary. It was still safe to go inside in 1966, and the kitchen was still standing. Mark went inside the big house and took a color photograph looking into the doorway of the kitchen. At the time, nothing seemed remarkable. It was after the photograph was developed and printed that he got quite the surprise. In the photograph is the transparent figure of a little girl. She has a long dress, an apron and long hair. The figure floats in the dark interior, standing in the kitchen.

Mark Cole Jr. did not believe in ghosts and thought the figure might be light on the chimney. Although to add to the strangeness, he has an

The Anthony Cole House in 2023.

1890 photograph of his father standing in a group of people, including a little girl eight to ten years old. She looks remarkably like the ghost in his photograph. Her identification is a mystery. He got this photo from his father's sister.

Cole's photograph and story were published in the October 31, 1985 *Durham Sun* newspaper. But in black-and-white newsprint it is difficult to make out the details. I saw a print of the original photograph in the 1990s, and it looked for all the world like there is a transparent girl inside the house. This was before technology was readily available to copy or scan such images, so we did not obtain a copy for the park. I don't particularly believe in ghosts either and have been at the Cole house many times, even at night, and never seen anything stranger than a flying squirrel.

# The Haunting: McCown-Mangum House

## *Early 1980s*

One of the first things encountered when visiting West Point on the Eno (Durham City Park) is a quaint restored 1840s farmhouse. This is the McCown-Mangum house. The house was built by John Cabe McCown, a onetime owner of the West Point Mill. The basement is the park office, and the top floor has at times been quarters for a live-in volunteer caretaker. Other times, park caretakers have lived on the park in a motor home. Such was the case in the early 1980s when Avery and Lucille Williams ran the West Point Mill and took care of the house. Their motor home was parked within sight of the house, and they often went in at night to shower and cook.

There are a couple of other characters in this story. Presley J. "PJ" Mangum bought the McCown house in 1891 and moved to West Point. PJ was an early Durham postmaster. His son Hugh was a notable photographer who shot images throughout the Southeast that serve as important historical documentation today. In 1893, sixteen-year-old Hugh moved into the house with his father. There were Mangums living in the house until 1968, when it was abandoned.

With clever maneuvering by the Eno River Association, the McCown-Mangum House was saved from a plan to bulldoze it, and soon after the house was deserted, West Point on the Eno Park was born and the house

The McCown-Mangum House.

restored. About a dozen years later, Avery and Lucille Williams were on-site caretakers.

As Avery told it, nearly every night, he heard ghostly creaks and bumps in the house. This would be easy to dismiss as the settling of an old house except for the other occurrences. Caretaker duties included securing and locking up the house at night. This included locking the door between the kitchen and dining room, carefully confirming it was secure. The house alarm was set, outer doors locked, and the Williamses would return to their motor home with key in pocket. Yet time and time again, when they reopened the house, the kitchen door was unlocked. The Williamses put the responsibility of the unlocked door on long departed Hugh Mangum. But that was only because they found a trunk filled with his old photographs in the house. But Hugh was not the only guilty party.

Lucille was meticulous in caring for the house. This included making the even longer departed PJ Mangum's bed, neat, even and no wrinkles, to look good for park visitors. She made it right and would leave, only to come back later and find the bed covers were wrinkled and out of line. Lucille would straighten it, leave, return and find it out of line again. Apparently, PJ thought this was funny.

Do the hauntings continue? Maybe you can find out. The McCown-Mangum House is open for tours by appointment and can be reserved for small gatherings. You could check the kitchen lock and make sure PJ's bed is made.

# 4

# THE DEADLY ENO

## One Shift Too Many

### Monday, March 1, 1852

West Point Mill is arguably the most successful and enduring of the more than thirty water-powered mills that operated on the Eno. It was in commercial operation from 1778 to 1942. The mill went through a variety of owners, with the name changing with each new owner. It also changed purposes. Most of the time it was grinding grain, but there were periods it operated as a sawmill.

In 1852 it was known as Sims' Sawmill, owned by the widow Rachel Sims. On this particular Monday, the mill was in operation, turning logs into lumber. The logs rode on rails held up by "sleepers," horizontal timbers like crossties on a railroad. Typically, the sleepers were three or more feet apart.

Walter Proctor was a nineteen-year-old mill employee, known to be a person of good character. He was sitting straddle on the long log being fed into the saw blade while chatting with the African American slave who was a mill attendant. Walter was careful, facing the blade to stay out of the obvious danger. As the log went deeper into the blade, he would shift his seat backward to avoid furiously spinning iron teeth. He was never aware when he reached the end of the log and made one last fatal shift backward. As

West Point Mill.

Walter fell off the log, the attendant tried to catch him, but Walter fell too fast. He fell through the sleepers and into the "pit." The pit is where large gears and giant belts, the mechanics of the mill, were whirring and spinning, turning the works inside the mill building.

The attendant reacted with all urgency to jerk the lever, shutting off the water to stop the waterwheel, robbing power from the machinery below. It was too late. Mangled and bruised, Walter died moments after being pulled out. Walter Proctor forever departed the Eno River valley, leaving behind his parents, a brother and a sister. An article in the *Hillsborough Recorder* referred to the tragedy as a "melancholy accident."

*In 1978, the West Point Mill was restored and put back into operation grinding grain for the education and enjoyment of visitors to West Point on the Eno City Park. It was a major project of the Eno River Association in partnership with Durham Parks and Recreation. It is open at scheduled times with millers to answer questions and tell mill stories. Pay respects to Walter Proctor when you visit, and pay attention to the millers when they tell you where it is safe and where it is not.*

# Never Going Home

## *Friday, February 7, 1873*

Jim Guess worked for W.W. Guess at the Guess Mill. Despite his name, Jim was not an owner or in the Guess family. As an African American, he was most likely a former slave that stayed on as an employee after the Civil War. It was common for former slaves to assume the last name of those who once enslaved them.

The mill was on the south side of the Eno River, and Jim lived on the north side. Today this is known as the Open Air Camp area of Eno River State Park, backing up to residential neighborhoods. A tall stone dam across the river formed the millpond that was between Jim's house and the mill. The dam held back deep water for over three-quarters of a mile of river.

Jim had a johnboat that he used to cross the millpond going back and forth between work and home. On the evening of February 7, Jim was rowing home from work when the dam broke loose without warning. The massive gush of water swept him away. The damage to the dam was severe. Jim and his boat were never found.

The river flows around the remains of the old Guess Mill dam.

*Millstones, earthworks and a stone chimney of the Guess Mill can be seen on the Laurel Bluffs Trail, just upstream from the Guess Road Bridge over the Eno. Hike the trail 330 yards upriver, and you can see the milldam. It was repaired after 1873, and the mill continued operation. A flood in 1893 and the great flood of 1908 also took out the dam, and each time it was rebuilt. In the 1940s, then owner Dr. George Johnson dynamited the dam in fear someone would drown in the pond. The dam still stands but with a big piece missing and the river running around it on the south side.*

# He Will Be Missed and Remembered

## Saturday, July 26, 1890

He built many brick structures around his hometown of Hillsborough and throughout the state of North Carolina. He manufactured one million bricks for the Duke & Company tobacco factories. In 1883, he was the superintendent of construction for Swain Memorial Hall at the University of North Carolina at Chapel Hill.

Seventy-seven-year-old Captain Henry Richards was more than just a stellar brick mason. He was a member of the historic Hillsborough Presbyterian Church and a Mason of Eagle Lodge 71 on King Street. He was an active leader of the local YMCA and played the piano to boot. One of his sons was a Hillsborough town commissioner. Captain Richards mattered to a lot of people. He was described as a man of sterling integrity, well beloved by everyone who knew him and appreciated as a friend and neighbor. In 1890, he was one of the oldest and most respected citizens of the town.

Henry Richards's marker at Hillsborough Presbyterian Church.

Henry Richards was never in the Confederate army, and we don't know where the title "Captain" came from, but it was how people knew him. With all he accomplished, Captain Richards also had some hard times. His son Roscoe died in 1867. Another son, also a bricklayer, died eighteen years later. For the last two years, Richards had been in failing health.

On a July afternoon, Captain Richards left for a walk along the Eno. He didn't return when expected, and folks went looking for him. His cane was found beside the river, purposely stuck straight up in the ground. His hat hung from the top of the cane. A search commenced, and at ten o'clock the next morning, his body was found in the river. A self-inflicted death was presumed. It appeared he walked into the river and submerged himself, never to draw another breath.

Crepe paper for mourning was hung on the homeplace doorknob. Inside, his wife, Eliza; two daughters; and last living son were in grief. Captain Richards was buried with Masonic honors in the family plot in the Hillsborough Presbyterian Church cemetery, where his tombstone reads, "Sacred to the Memory."

# Gloom Descends on Fairntosh

## Monday, April 4, 1892

North Carolina's largest plantation, Fairntosh, was still owned by the Cameron family in 1892. Cameron's Red Mill served the agricultural needs of the plantation and was located on the Eno a short distance upstream from the modern-day Red Mill Road Bridge. A dam across the river provided a long, deep millpond to power the waterwheel. On April 4, the current owner, Bennehan Cameron, was in Raleigh, planning to be there for a few days.

John and Corinna Glenn and their nine-year-old son resided on the plantation. Likely they were tenant farmers, a common situation in the post–Civil War South. At that time on the Eno, many people were subsistence farmers; their needs were met by the land, the river and hard work. Fishing on the river wasn't recreation—it was food gathering. The Glenns had set nets in the millpond, and around five o'clock in the evening Corinna and her son went down to check and see if they caught any fish.

The hour got late, and the pair had not returned home. Fear for their safety spread across the plantation, and the residents instituted a search of the property. It took hours to find Corinna's bonnet on the riverbank. Now the searchers were concerned this might be a drowning. On the bank, bushes torn out by the roots made it look like someone was holding on to those

Cameron's Red Mill dam made the river wider and deeper here. History repeats today as Falls Lake backs up into the Eno.

bushes when they gave way. A large amount of hair was in the bushes like someone had grabbed a head full of it trying to pull someone else from the water. The ground was scuffed up with fresh dirt as from a struggle. Their speculation was either Corinna or her son fell in and the other tried to pull the first one out while holding on to the bushes, then fell in themselves when the bushes broke free.

The searchers resorted to dragging the river. About four o'clock in the morning, anxiety became reality: Corinna's body was found and retrieved from the river. A telegram was sent to Colonel Cameron in Raleigh, informing him of the situation. He returned to the plantation by train late in the day. Meanwhile, the search for the boy went all night. Come the morning light, his body was found on the river bottom, not far from where they found his mom.

No inquest was held, as the coroner, Dr. Johnson, said the evidence did not warrant one. The mood of the many residents of the plantation was cast in quite a gloom.

*Cameron's Red Mill was about a mile upstream from the headwater of the Neuse River, which is the junction of the Eno and Flat Rivers. This is public land now, managed by the U.S. Army Corps of Engineers and North Carolina Wildlife Resources Commission. The Mountains to Sea Trail passes by on the south bank of the river.*

From Occoneechee Mountain, you can look down on the Eno.

# Does Anyone Remember?

## *September 8, 1900*

In 1900, it was the Occoneechee Mountains, not the one mountain we visit today. This was before one whole mountain was mined to nothingness for the valuable manufacturing mineral pyrophyllite. On an early fall Saturday, an eight-year-old little boy drowned in the Eno River at the foot of the Occoneechee Mountains. Many North Carolina newspapers carried this snippet and nothing more. None told us who he was or how it happened, not even the *Orange County Observer* in Hillsborough.

# No Answer at Bob Hole

## *Sunday, July 7, 1901*

The circumstances of Sam Miller's death remain a mystery. Was it an accident? Was it suicide? Was it murder?

The Bob Hole.

Miller was found in the Bob Hole on Sunday afternoon, drowned. It is not what the young men who came there to swim were expecting. Bob Hole was, and is, a popular summer cooling place. These days, people access it from the Dunnagan or Pump Station Trails in Eno River State Park.

Sam Miller lived alone in an out of the way hut. He had no known relatives. And he had been in the illicit whiskey business most of his life. He had a police record for ignoring internal revenue liquor laws. Recently, he had been arrested by federal officers and did some jail time. About two or three weeks before he passed away, he was somehow unexpectedly able to post bond and was released. Surprising, unless you figure the federal agents had reason to show some leniency. Miller had turned informant and was providing the government a lot of good information. This should have been kept quiet, but after his release, rumors were flying among area whiskey dealers that he might be "giving the crowd away."

Miller was seen alive Saturday night. Authorities believed he went to his still on Sunday morning, where he either died by suicide or was drowned in the river by his enemies. The body was extricated from the river and taken to his hut on Sunday night. There were no markings or evidence of foul play on him. Finding no evidence to suggest a crime, Durham County coroner

Maddry did not deem an inquest necessary. He did try to be thorough and made two trips to Bob Hole searching for evidence on July 7 and 8. The afternoon of the eighth, Miller was buried at the county's expense.

Was it an accident, suicide or murder? It is true there were no marks of a struggle on his body. It is also true that Bob Hole is not deep. Nowadays it is at best waist deep. While it may be possible it was deeper in 1901, it's hard to imagine it was too deep for Miller to stand up with his head above water. Bob Hole was downstream from the Durham Pumping Station Dam and too far upstream for the Guess Mill Dam backwater, so no man-made structures raised the water level. Unless he had a medical incident that rendered him unconscious, it is hard to believe it was an accident. But for it to be a suicide it would mean Miller walked out in the river and held himself underwater in a depth he could stand. It's difficult to imagine he could force himself to stay under, but not impossible, as this has happened more than once on the Eno. That leaves murder as the most likely scenario. There was motive and opportunity but a lack of evidence and thus a lack of answers at Bob Hole.

# Grief Comes to Christian's Mill

### Sunday, August 4, 1901

In 1901, West Point Mill was known as Christian's Mill, one of several names it had over seventeen decades of commercial operation. It also varied operations between a gristmill and a sawmill. One thing was consistent: young folks always enjoyed swimming in the millpond during the heat of the summer.

A dam taller than a man's head spanned the Eno River, forming the millpond and backing up the river for nearly half a mile. Gates diverted water out of the millpond to the mill wheel four hundred feet down river. The pond was deep and refreshing, which is why on this Sunday morning Beleah Rigsbee, Gene Dossett, Charley Rhew and a few other friends were in the water having a great time. Beleah, about twenty-four years old, probably knew this place well. His homeplace was a couple miles away on Guess Road, where his father still lived.

There was a big rock out in the middle surrounded by twelve feet deep water. The men were swimming out to the rock, climbing up and jumping

West Point, formerly Christian's Mill dam, in 2024.

back in. Charley Rhew was watching as Beleah swam out, but short of the rock Beleah sank and did not resurface. Rhew called for help, and the other swimmers began an immediate search. There was a crew building the new Roxboro Road Bridge just past the mill, and they came to help. About noon, Tim Thompson of the bridge construction crew dove down, found Beleah and brought him out with his soul departed.

The body was carried to his father's house. He was buried the next day in the family plot. No one knew why Beleah sank. Observers speculated cramps or heart failure. He was overweight and had been complaining about trouble around his heart. Surviving Beleah were his father, brother, sister and his fiancée, Emma Taylor, who was described as almost crazed with grief. Her reaction was perfectly understandable.

*The* Durham Sun *newspaper took this opportunity to warn young men about exerting themselves in the water and expressed this warning particularly applied to swimming on a Sunday. While that may seem callous, they may have been on to something. Of twenty-three unintentional Eno drownings we know of, ten were on a Sunday. No other day of the week has more than three.*

# Double Death at Hall Millpond

## *Sunday, May 21, 1905*

On a fine spring day, five young people were having a good time strolling along the Hall Millpond on the Eno River near Efland.

Lacy Hughes, twenty-seven years old, was well known and well connected, a successful owner of two stores within the Hughes and Cooper Mercantile corporation, also near Efland. He grew up in nearby Cedar Grove, the son of the late Dr. Hughes.

Earl Faucette was in his late teens or early twenties. News reports gave three different ages. This would not be the only confusion in the reporting of this incident. He also was a Cedar Grove local and a graduate of the Cedar Grove Academy and a student at the North Carolina Agricultural and Mechanical College (North Carolina State University). He also was prominently connected and reported to be a bright specimen of moral and physical manhood.

Neither Faucette nor Hughes were married, which explains why they were escorting the three ladies. Eloise Brown of Salem, Virginia, was a music teacher at Cedar Grove Academy. Rounding out the group were Earl's sister Maud and Eloise's sister Bessie.

About 2:00 p.m. the group found an old boat. Lacy, Earl and Eloise got in and began quietly rowing about the pond. Suddenly and inexplicably the boat capsized and sank. As the threesome hit the water, Lacy put his arms around Eloise and told her, "Don't be afraid, I will save you."

On shore, Maud and Bessie saw the tragedy unfolding and screamed for help. Doc Cates, who was working at the mill, heard the cries, came running and immediately jumped in and saved Eloise. She was about fifteen feet from the bank, floating in water twelve feet deep. At first Eloise was thrashing and bobbing, but in the short time it took Cates to reach her, she was floating listlessly. Cates took hold and began pulling her back to shore. Suddenly, Eloise became agitated and began to pull him underwater in her panic. It appeared both would drown, but Cates got them close enough to the bank that onlookers were able to push a pole out to them, which he readily grabbed, and the folks pulled them to safety. Eloise lost consciousness and did not come to until nine hours later.

Earl and Lacy were considered expert swimmers, and everyone ashore expected them to surface and swim to safety. That didn't happen. A search of the pond ensued, and about fifty people gathered to help or gawk. It was about 5:00 p.m. when their bodies were found, each about ten feet away from the two opposite banks. Even though the men had been under the river's surface for hours, bystanders and doctors tried to revive them. Eventually, Dr. Terrell of Cedar Grove pronounced them beyond human aid.

Pelham Faucette of Salem, Earl's brother, arrived the next day to take responsibility of Earl's earthly body. Lacy left behind his mother, four brothers and three sisters. Burial of both occurred in family plots on May 25 with large attendance.

One report was made the boat was recovered and found with no defect. Another report called the boat old and rotten. Regardless, it was apparent the mythological Charon was at the helm, ferrying two men to the afterlife way too soon.

*Hall Mill was on the Eno River a short distance downstream from the confluence of the East and West Forks of the Eno and north of Efland. Modern-day Hall Mill Road crosses the river near the site. Cedar Grove Academy on Carr Store Road, between the East and West Forks of the Eno, began operation before 1845 and closed in 1915.*

# No Escape from Devil's Sinkhole

## Sunday, August 25, 1907

East of Hillsborough, downstream from Lawrence Road and south of Saint Mary's Road, there is a place on the Eno River known as the Devil's Sinkhole. It's a beautiful spot with a rocky cascade of river flowing down between boulders into a wide hole. In 1907, the north side was rolling green farmland. The south bank was and is made up of tall, steep hills covered in mountain laurel with large gray rock outcrops at each end of the hole. The sinkhole is not particularly deep, not so that you would expect someone to drown. The center is over a man's head, but twenty feet in any direction it becomes shallow enough to stand. Maybe it was deeper in 1907. The river would have been dammed above the sinkhole to create a millpond to drive Berry's Public Mill for grinding corn and sawing timber. The charming mill with its stone and timber walls was on the north side not far up the riverbank within sight of the sinkhole.

On August 25, John Pickett went swimming at Berry's Mill with his friend Jasper "Cot" Cotrell and John's father, Sidney. This was one year

The author in the Devil's Sinkhole. *Photo by Fred Myers.*

to the day before the great flood of 1908 that wiped out most of the mills and dams on the Eno. They got there about noon and enjoyed a couple of hours of refreshing in the river within standing depth. Then twenty-two-year-old John waded farther into the cool river, following Cot, who took some strokes out into the deep water. John couldn't swim and unwittingly followed and was swallowed into the depths of the sinkhole.

Cot made a desperate effort to save the panic-stricken John. Grabbing his friend led to a violent struggle as he tried to hold on. It came down to saving himself. Cot broke free and with a few strokes swam to shore. Having failed to save John, he ran to the nearest house to call for help. John Pickett's body was recovered from the sinkhole about 4:00 p.m., ninety minutes after he went down. His funeral was held the next day at New Sharon Methodist Church, two miles from the Devil's Sinkhole. If you go to New Sharon to visit him, there is no grave marker. If there ever was a stone, time has erased it.

*The Devil's Sinkhole is tough to get to. The south side of the river is state park, but no trail or road comes close, and it is more than three miles from the nearest parking lot. The north side is private property, and trespassing is actively discouraged. However, in the winter, from the state park side you can look across the river and see the stone wall remains of the old Berry Public Mill. In August 2022, 115 years after John Pickett drowned, I carefully measured the depth of the hole and found it to be nine feet, three inches at its deepest.*

# Great Sadness at Hall Mill

## Saturday, February 15, 1908

Five-year-old Cary Spivey lived near the old Hall Mill on the Eno River with his father and younger brother. On a winter Saturday, with the river swiftly flowing, Cary was playing on a small bridge over the tailrace, using a stick to measure the depth of the water rushing below his feet. Leaning out too far, he slipped and fell in headfirst and was carried by the force of the water down the race into the Eno in water described as eight to ten feet deep.

Cary's little brother saw the fall and yelled for help. But Cary sank into the winter-cold water before help could reach him.

It was difficult to find the body. The water was frigid and swift. Darkness descends early in February. Yet the search was kept up all night by neighbors. It was three o'clock the next afternoon before young Cary was found, about a mile downriver from where he fell in. He was interred at the family burial ground near their home.

*Hall Mill is long gone but was on the Eno River a short distance downstream from the confluence of the East and West Forks of the Eno about four miles northwest of Hillsborough. Tailraces are the usually short channel for water to pass from the mill wheel back into the river.*

# Death Net

## Thursday, June 11, 1908

A good-sized group of people were seining the Eno late morning. For those unfamiliar, seining catches fish by dragging a wide net across the river and pinning the fish up against the bank. Another option is to spread the net across the river, usually in rushing water, and a group wades the river downstream herding fish into the net, which is folded up and the fish are trapped inside. Typically, seining happens in deeper areas, where the bigger fish are. In this group was twenty-year-old Waylon McLeod. He was a tinner by trade.

The river was rushing pretty good as McLeod worked his end of the net. Under the surface, his shoe brushed the net and a simple shoestring eyelet caught in the mesh. The force of the water combined with the pull on the net tripped him up and dragged him underwater. Struggling to the surface, McLeod called for help, and several people jumped to his rescue. W.H. Matthews and his fifteen-year-old son Callie grasped McLeod, but his frantic struggling pulled both of them under. W.H. was able to wrench Callie loose from McLeod's grasp and carry him to safety while McLeod went down for the last time.

The seine was drawn to the bank, pulling the unresponsive McLeod, his foot still entangled in the net. All efforts to resuscitate him were fruitless. Twenty-five men and women witnessed the accident, and the consensus was he was submerged no more than two minutes. The corner was notified, and his body brought to the medical examiner's office. No water was found in his lungs. The supposition was that while McLeod was trapped underwater, the terror of the circumstances resulted in a heart attack and he died.

McLeod's body was shipped to his home in Harnett County for funeral and burial.

# Tragic Sunday on Geer Millpond

## Sunday, June 28, 1914

Things were going well for twenty-year-old Walter Faulkner. Three months prior, he had moved from Henderson, North Carolina, to Durham. He got a job at the Erwin Mill over on the Hillsborough Road making denim. He was living in west Durham in the Erwin Mill village at Mrs. Gilliam's boardinghouse. The people who worked with him at the mill had a lot of good to say about him and his work ethic.

On this June Sunday afternoon, Walter and two friends were heading for a different kind of mill, a grinding mill on the Eno River. It was the Guess Mill built in 1848, which had been known as the Geer Mill since 1874, when Squire William Guess sold out to Fred Geer. Of the many Eno River mills destroyed by the great flood of 1908, it was the only one built back, dam restored, and continued commercial operation. Walter and his two buddies James Strawburg and Pell Culberson tried to hire a horse and spring wagon, but finding this impossible, they hiked the five miles to the Geer Mill.

Arriving at the mill, they waded the shallow river below the milldam, crossing to the north bank, and then headed upstream, where they changed into their swimwear. James was a poor swimmer and chose to wade in the shallows. Walter and Pell jumped in about a dozen feet upstream of the dam, swam across the pond and back again. Just twenty feet from returning to the riverbank, Pell saw a slight spasm pass over Walter. Walter called for help, and Pell swam back to grab him, and they went into a clinch. The struggling pair sank twelve feet to the bottom of the river. Pell did what he didn't want to do but had to do. He kicked himself free of Walter and then swam quick strokes to the surface. Treading water, he waited for Walter to appear so he could drag him to safety by his hair. But the sun wasn't going to shine on Walter's living face.

James saw the drama unfold. He and Pell marked the spot where Walter went down by observing the shade of a tree over the river. James ran to a neighboring house and phoned Sheriff Harward, who came with all deliberate speed to the mill with a rescue party.

The rescue party arrived before dark. However, it did not occur to anyone that the earth was moving and with it the angle of the sun. The marking shade of the tree moved with the sun, and the rescuers were diving in the wrong place. Night fall comes late in June, and the rescue party put in long hours, until it was too dark to continue safely. Plans were made to return Monday morning.

Before the sheriff and rescuers could return, a crowd of boys arrived early and resumed the search. By the time the sheriff got there about 9:30 a.m., the boys had found Walter and were bringing his body to shore in a rowboat that was kept at the pond. Walter's earthly remains were taken to Durham by Sheriff Harward, where he had the sad duty of calling Walter's father in Henderson. The body was shipped home the same day.

With no evidence of foul play, the coroner ruled the death an accident. Pell and James were described as devastated by their friend's drowning. Pell was recognized as a hero in the community for trying to save Walter at his own peril and then staying to help with the recovery.

*Three-quarters of the Geer Mill Dam stands to this day. From the Laurel Bluffs Trail in Eno River State Park, ensconced in the beauty of the river and forest, you can see the tragic spot where Walter Faulkner took his last breath.*

# First and Last Swim at Christian's Mill

## Sunday, August 13, 1916

It was a Sunday in August, and it was hot. Eleven boys from Durham bicycled out to Christian's Mill, which we now know as West Point. W.J. Christian owned and operated the mill from 1888 to 1909. Even though he had sold it seven years earlier, it was still known as Christian's. This was one of the few mills on the Eno River to survive the great flood of 1908.

Among the gang of eleven was a newcomer. Nineteen-year-old Wade Freeman had moved from Winston-Salem to Durham only a week prior. He took a job at Liggett and Myers Tobacco as a machine operator, having prior experience doing the same in his hometown. Wade found boarding at the home of Mrs. Beaman on Rigsbee Avenue. He made friends quickly; hence he was now with a large group of local boys who brought him to this great swimming spot.

Swimming, jumping and splashing in the millpond, they were having a big time. By one o'clock all but Wade, tired of swimming, had emerged from the river and were dressing. Wade Freeman, alone in the river, suddenly and silently slipped from view. Three of his new swimming buddies—Robert Cole, S.F. Hedgepath and N.J. Renby—valiantly attempted rescue with dozens of dives, but the water was too deep. Finally, Robert climbed about fifteen feet up an overhanging tree and dove. The momentum carried him down deep enough to grab Wade. By then, Wade had been underwater about fifteen minutes.

With assistance from Hegepath and Renby, they were able to drag the dead weight of Wade ashore, limp and eyes fixed. The body got considerably banged up from bushes and rocks as it was dragged from the water. Efforts made to resuscitate Wade failed. He had been submerged too long. Transportation by car was found, and several of the young men drove to Durham to notify the sheriff and coroner. Hall and Wynn Funeral Home came out to the river to retrieve the body.

Wade's remains were shipped by train to Ulah, North Carolina, where he had a brother. Two of the would-be rescuers, Robert Cole and S.F. Hedgepath, accompanied the body. Even though they had known Wade less than a week, they wished to show respect. Wade Freeman was considered a good swimmer. The consensus was that overexertion led to his drowning, exacerbated by cycling from Durham over hot, dusty roads.

The Eno River was dammed to form Lake Ben Johnston to provide water for the Hillsborough, at the site of the old Dimmock's Mill.

# Found at Dimmocks Mill

## 1924

Local newspaper records from this decade are scant, so we don't know much about J.H. Murry. He disappeared on a Friday morning. A search for him went on all night. He was found on Saturday morning, dead in the Eno River near Dimmocks Mill.

*Dimmocks Mill started out as Taylor's Mill in 1817. It went through a variety of owners, and Edwin Dimmock owned it from only 1876 to 1883, but his name stuck, as evidenced by Dimmocks Mill Road in Hillsborough. The mill was at the junction of the Eno and Seven Mile Creek, where Lake Ben Johnston and King's Highway Park are now. The mill was still standing when J.H. Murry drowned, but it was no longer in service.*

# Fishing No More

## *Sunday, May 28, 1939*

Mildred Crank was an eighteen-year-old Bragtown High School student from Durham, just days away from graduation. On a Sunday she went fishing with Carl Browning and his two children: Marie, fourteen, and James, twelve. This was down on the lower Eno in eastern Durham County, just below the old YMCA camp in the Mount Hebron Church community. Shortly before noon, Carl went to a nearby filling station to buy ice cream for everyone. Meanwhile, Mildred, Marie, and James went wading. Mildred couldn't see the bottom well, and without warning, she stepped abruptly into a six-foot-deep hole. Mildred had never learned to swim. Both James and Marie were swimmers, and they struggled mightily to pull Mildred to safety, but they were not strong enough. In the frenzy, Mildred pulled Marie under, but Marie was able to pull free and get back into shallow water. The children were wearing swimsuits, but Mildred was wearing coveralls. The weight of the wet coveralls dragged her down like a rock. Carl returned with the ice cream to find his children frantic and Mildred gone. He notified Durham Sheriff "Cat" Belvin, who responded to the scene with ABC officer Tom Wilkie. On his first dive, Wilkie found Mildred's body, about an hour after the drowning. Despite the elapsed time, they still tried to revive her, but to no avail. She was buried at Pine Hill Cemetery (now Woodlawn Memorial Park) in Durham two days later. Her death compounded family tragedies, as it followed the death of Mildred's father a year before in car wreck on Durham's Hillsborough Road.

*Bragtown High School merged with Mangum High School in 1952 to form Northern High School, one of two Durham high schools in the Eno River watershed.*

# Independence Day Will Never Be the Same

## *Friday, July 4, 1952*

Yearby Street in Durham is now on the Duke University Campus. In July 1952, it was the neighborhood where seventeen-year-old Louis McDaniel lived. Louis was a rising senior at Durham High School, where he was a three-letter athlete in football, basketball and baseball. This summer he was pitching American Legion ball and had a game in Graham scheduled for the next day. At more than six feet tall and 180 pounds, Louis batted .450 and also played first base. His American Legion coach said he had pro potential. One more thing to know about him: Louis never learned to swim.

On July 4, Louis went on a picnic and fishing expedition to the Eno with his friends Charles Johnson, Norman Pendergrass and Weldon Cheek. They went down through the woods behind the prison camp on Guess Road. Back then, the land on the river was owned by the state Department of Corrections. After eating a watermelon, the teenagers decided to go wading. This was about 4:20 p.m., and the shallow Eno is mostly a safe place to wade.

Most of the river may be safe to wade, but there are places in the Eno where it is too deep to see the bottom, hiding hazards natural to a free-flowing river. Louis never knew the deep hole was there until he stepped into it, disappearing with his hands waving. Norman and Charles weren't great swimmers, but they still searched frantically for their friend. Weldon couldn't swim at all and stayed out of the deep water, astutely not becoming a second victim.

After twenty minutes of diving for Louis, Norman ran a mile through the woods for help. The volunteer Durham Lifesaving Corps arrived within fifteen minutes of the call. The three friends stood quietly by in their swimsuits, one of them holding a fishing pole, while the divers did their work. The teen with the pole kept repeating, "We did our best." Fifty-five minutes after Louis went down, following several dives, Fred Christian found the body. Members of the Lifesaving Corps took turns administering artificial respiration.

Responders from the fire department and sheriff's deputies arrived soon after Louis was recovered. County coroner Dr. R.A. Horton pronounced him dead at 5:50 p.m. Lonnie Henner was able to drive a jeep back through the woods to collect the blanket-wrapped body and carry it to the funeral home. A celebration of life was held the following Sunday at Greystone Baptist Church, and Louis is buried in Maplewood Cemetery. Members of the Durham High School and American Legion baseball teams took part in the service. Their game in Graham was postponed out of respect.

# Deep Losses at Synnott Hole

## 1963 and 2019

*Synnott Hole is deep, a natural hole in the Eno River. In two areas below and on either side of the island at the top, its depth exceeds twelve feet. In 2020, I carefully measured the hole and found that at its deepest it is twelve feet, seven inches. Stunning beauty and swimmable depths have drawn the community for generations.*

### Sunday, May 19, 1963

In 1963, the deep water in what would one day become West Point on the Eno City Park was at the Synnott Hole. The dam that gives us deep water today was broke through in 1942 and not rebuilt until the West Point Mill was restored in 1976.

On this Sunday, thirteen-year-old Ronald Dement, his twin brother, Donald, and their friend Monty Gravitte came from Durham to the Synnott Hole to swim and have fun, like many before them, like so many after them. Sadly, this was Ronald's last swim. In the deep water, he started floundering. Donald did his best to rescue his brother, but Ronald was pulling him under.

The Synnott Hole.

Donald wrenched free, made it safely back to the bank and looked back, and Ronald was gone. Monty ran to a nearby store to call for help.

Two divers from the Durham County Rescue Squad began searching shortly after 5:00 p.m. Durham Sheriff's deputies and the Durham Fire Department assisted with the search and recovery. An hour later, the divers found Ronald's body. Left to grieve were his parents, two sisters and five brothers.

## Wednesday, May 15, 2019

Four days shy of the fifty-sixth anniversary of Ronald Dement's drowning, Karriem Ahmad "Eric" Jenkins went swimming at the Synnott Hole. Eric was an accomplished student, class valedictorian of the Middle College of NC A&T, and was now at UNC-CH, where he was a junior in psychology and biology. He was a gifted orator. As early as the seventh grade, he won his first Sunday school oratorical contest for churches spanning across Winston-Salem and from then on kept winning. Eric was a determined person who couldn't be told he wasn't capable of doing something. Family remembers him as a free spirit and an unstoppable force. At UNC, he involved himself in several social justice causes.

It was a little after three o'clock, in the hot of the afternoon. Eric was swimming across Synnott Hole with friends, going from one end to the other. He told nearby Carla Beachem that he was tired. She asked him if he could make it across and he said, "No." She tried to help, but Eric panicked, and every time she grabbed him, he pushed Carla under. She broke free. Eric struggled a few more seconds and then sank. He was pulled out, resuscitated and transported to Duke Hospital but the effort proved futile. He died in the hospital the next day. A celebration of Karriem Ahmad "Eric" Jenkins life was held in his hometown, Greensboro, on May 21.

# Beware the Bobbitt

## Thursday–Saturday, July 12–14, 1973

The iconic Bobbitt Hole is a mysterious and beautiful place. At more than eighteen feet, it is the deepest spot in the Eno River. The river enters the

The Bobbitt Hole.

hole going northwest and turns sharply to exit northeast. Large boulders guard the entrance and south bank. "Bobbitt" is a derivative of the name of a supernatural being believed to inhabit dark mysterious holes in creeks and rivers in Essex, England (where there are six Bobbitt Holes). Early colonials from Essex probably saw the Eno's Bobbitt Hole as likely to also house this mythical creature and transposed the name.

From the first Paleo-Indians to explore the Eno up to today, teenage boys have sought the clear, cooling river water on hot summer days, which is why on a July day friends Mike Hagwood and Jack Evans Jr. hiked five hundred yards through the woods down from Sparger Road to the Bobbitt Hole. Jack lived on Sparger and Mike just a few blocks away. Both sixteen, they were students at Northern High School. Normally, the Eno flows with a mild current. But when Mike and Jack arrived about noon, the river was up, running strong, high and swift from the previous day's thunderstorms. The usual clear water was stirred up to chocolate-milk brown. Undeterred, they dove in from the large rocks at the top of the hole into the fast-moving water.

Jack swiftly swam out of the strong current into a quiet eddy. No longer in the river's grip, he looked back and saw Mike struggling against the force of the moving water. Mike bobbed on the surface as he tried to fight the current and reach the riverbank. The expression on his face made it clear he was in trouble. Jack's attempts to rescue Mike were heroic. He swam to Mike and let him grab his arm. But Mike was panicked, grabbed Jack by the neck and climbed on his shoulders while hitting and beating his would-be savior. Jack was able to break free and swam back to shore, seeking a stick or log, something to reach out and save his friend, but he couldn't find anything. Out of options, he ran the five hundred yards back up a path to the nearest house to call for help. Jack returned promptly, but Mike had disappeared.

Rescue squads and sheriff's deputies from Durham and Orange Counties responded to search for Mike. Along with volunteers, more than fifty people searched eight hours using johnboats and inflatable rafts and walking the banks, stopping only when night overshadowed the river.

The rescue squads and deputies returned early Friday and searched until 6:00 p.m. They were hampered by the still rain-swollen and murky river. Divers searched the hole. Rescuers on foot searched under the theory the strong current may have carried Mike away to wash up on downstream riverbanks. Durham County sheriff Marvin Davis searched overhead by airplane for four hours. It was not until the third day of the search, Saturday, shortly before noon, that responders were able to return Mike to his family. Using drag lines, the Orange County Rescue Squad found him fifteen feet below the Eno surface. He had not traveled, found just below where he jumped in.

On July 16, he was memorialized at Durham's Liberty Free Will Baptist Church and interred at the New Hope Christian Church cemetery in Franklin County.

*I always heard Bobbitt Hole was eighteen feet deep and in August 2020 confirmed it myself at eighteen feet seven inches.*

# River Bones

## *Wednesday June 9–Wednesday, August 25, 1982*

*On the south bank of the Eno, at the end of Denfield Street, behind the Old Farm neighborhood, lies the old Nello Teer Rock Quarry. Now it is being allowed to fill with water as an emergency water source for Durham. In 1982, it was providing stone to the community.*

The Eno River adjacent to the Teer quarry.

Down below the Teer Quarry, a lone fisherman moved around casting his line from the bank of the Eno River. He was looking for the honey-hole, where the bream were congregated. What he found was both startling and sad, a human skeleton in the bushes.

It was about seven o'clock in the evening when the bones were found, ten feet from the water's edge. By the time the fisherman got to a phone and Durham Police sergeant Britt got there, dusk was threatening. Britt figured out he was beyond the northern city limits and turned it over to the sheriff's office. With the delays, it was dark when Chief State Medical Examiner R. Page Hudson got to the scene. Floodlights were set up on the riverbank for him to examine the skeleton. Cause of death couldn't be determined, but the police had a clue as to the identity. Thinking further investigation in daylight would be beneficial, Hudson decided to leave the skeleton overnight. Standard procedure is that an officer stays with the body all night, but news reports don't indicate who had that grim duty.

Medical Examiner Hudson and Durham Sheriff investigators were back in the morning. They could tell the person had been dead about two months. They weren't ready to declare whether the cause of death was natural, murder or suicide. They had a preliminary identification. Near the skeleton was a pair of pants, one leg tied to a tree. A wallet in a pocket had the identification card of Larry Osler Watkins.

Larry Watkins, who lived on Club Boulevard in Durham, was the owner/operator of Watkins Plumbing Company. He was forty-five years old. Watkins had last been seen by family on the morning of June 9 as he left his father's Hillsborough home to go to work. His van was found that night behind the old Bonanza restaurant on Roxboro Road. There was no trace of him until his wallet was found seventy-seven days later. Was this skeleton Larry Watkins?

The bones were taken to Chapel Hill for further investigation by the state medical examiner. Two days after the discovery, dental records confirmed this was Watkins, bringing both dismay and closure to his son, father, sisters and brothers. The belief of Examiner Hudson and the investigating officers was he hanged himself on the banks of the Eno on the day he disappeared. He was remembered at a memorial service on August 28.

What was it that pushed Larry Watkins over the edge, to do what most consider unthinkable and leave behind his family? While there is no way to know everything, one clue surfaced during the time he was missing. One month to the day after he disappeared, a legal notice appeared in the *Durham Morning Herald*. The Internal Revenue Service had confiscated his van and all the tools inside and were auctioning them off for unpaid federal taxes. Perhaps stress beyond his capacity sent him to the Eno.

# The Deep

## *1993, 2007, 2015, 2019*

*The deepest waters in the Eno River Valley are not Bobbitt or Synnott Holes. They are the old Nello Teer Quarry and the Eno Quarry. Both are very close to the river. At the Eno Quarry, you can look down into the quarry or the river from a single spot. The Eno Quarry was privately owned until acquired for Eno River State Park on Halloween in 2002. Stone was dug there for the construction of Interstate 85 from 1960 to 1964. After closing operations, the quarry slowly filled with water. Once full, it became a popular swimming hole. The owners did not want anyone there, but they could not control people slipping through the woods to swim. It was the property of the T.S. and Margaret Coile. In the past, when Mr. Coile was alive, they put "no trespassing signs" and a barbed-wire fence around the quarry, but both were always ignored. Signs disappeared in days, including a two-foot-by-four-foot one-hundred-dollar sign. Another time they hired a security guard who was insulted and cussed out by trespassers. In retaliation, someone spread roofing nails in the Coiles' driveway causing a half-dozen flat tires. So they let the security guard go. Once trespassers cut down their pasture fence, allowing sixty-four black Charolais cattle to get out. Rangers from the adjacent Eno River State Park would advise folks they weren't allowed at the quarry, but the common response was they knew and didn't care. It was lawless until the state park took over, built trails, put up signs and rangers patrolled. To this day, the Eno Quarry remains a popular recreation spot. It is sixty feet at its deepest, four acres of surface and unforgiving. There is precious little shallow water to stand in. Most banks are high and take above average dexterity to climb out. Rangers do not recommend swimming, and only strong swimmers should ever enter these waters.*

## Sunday, September 12, 1993

It was about 5:30 in the evening when Orange County 911 got the call from a dripping-wet and panting young man who knocked on Maxine Bandy's door asking to use the phone. Bandy lived in the Caroline Trailer Park across the street from the Cabelands parking lot in Eno River State

Eno Quarry.

Park. She assumed he had locked his keys in his car. Over the years, she had handed out about twenty-five coat hangers to people sneaking out to the Eno Quarry, who used the grass shoulders of her road (Howe Street) or the state park lot to leave their cars. This time was different. For the first time, there was a drowning in the old stone quarry.

Brian Glenn Wright was a dean's list Duke engineering student from Robbinsville, North Carolina. He grew up swimming in lakes. He was once certified as a lifeguard. At twenty-one years old, he had no health problems. On this Sunday, he and five friends hiked out to the Eno Quarry through the woods to go swimming. They were there without permission, but Brian was not a troublemaker. Friends said he probably did not know he was not supposed to be there. By 1993, most of the warning signs had been pulled off the trees and the fence beaten down.

Brian swam out into the quarry, sank down without warning and never came up. It was too far and too late for rescue. Responders attempted to drag for his body, but the bottom was too irregular to be effective. Durham County Sheriff's Office sent their dive team, which searched for three days. Divers had to grope because the loose sediment they stirred up on the bottom made visibility murky. Below the first few feet of surface, the water is very cold. Eight-hour days of searching in chilly water were exhausting and proving fruitless. U.S. Army divers searched another two days. The search was suspended after eight days. Brian's family was out there every day. And every day, Duke students, oblivious to what was going on, continued showing up to swim.

They never really gave up looking. Going forward was what is called a limited continuous search. This is when search teams train in an area where a body is believed to be in hopes of recovery. On Sunday, October 17, five weeks after Brian disappeared, a dive team from Madison County, North Carolina, found him. Groping on the bottom, a diver felt a crevice and reached down, where he felt Brian's body. It was so cold down there the body had been refrigerated and was not showing signs decomposition.

Brian lies under his tombstone in Wiggins Cemetery in Graham County, where his family still places flowers.


## Monday, July 9, 2007

It was almost fourteen years before the deep claimed another. Ian Creath of Chapel Hill had stayed home to go to college. He was a sophomore at the

University of North Carolina majoring in psychology. Ian was a talented writer and artist and an accomplished guitarist in the band Fallen September. Responsible and a hard worker, during high school he waited tables at Allan and Son Pit Cooked Barbecue out on Highway 86. The Eno Quarry was one of his favorite places on earth.

When warm weather came, Ian and his friends swam the quarry two to three times a week. It brought him great peace, and he wanted to share the experience with others. On this Monday, shortly before eight o'clock in the evening, Ian swam out into the quarry to retrieve a raft. Before he got there, he called for help. Friends swam after him, but Ian sank before they reached him. Other swimmers at the quarry tried to help find him, but visibility in the quarry doesn't extend past your toes.

Divers from Orange County Rescue arrived with only a short time before nightfall. They dove until it was too dark to be safe. It was great comfort to Ian's mother when we told her rangers would stay with Ian all night and would keep onlookers from coming near. Tuesday morning, divers from Durham County were at the quarry early to resume the search. They found his body about 9:00 a.m. He rests in the Chapel Hill Memorial Cemetery. His mother has visited the quarry on several occasions as a place of remembrance.

*In a twist of fate, I left the quarry at dark because Tuesday I was flying to New Mexico with nine teenage Boy Scouts, several from Chapel Hill. Unbeknownst to me, they were friends of Ian's and they learned of his death as I relayed the story on the airplane.*

## Thursday, July 23, 2015

An eighteen-foot red clay bluff was the hot jump spot of the Eno Quarry. It was not a sheer drop. To clear the bank and some stumps required a running start and no hesitation. If you cleared everything, it was a refreshing drop in deep, clear water. If you came up short, it meant serious injury and a ride in an ambulance, which happened several times each summer. This spot was a favorite of many a brave diver over decades. Lamont Marcell Burt Jr. was one of those divers. He was in great shape. He was a standout wrestler at Broughton High School in Raleigh, having been a conference champion and placed well in the state tournament. The seventeen-year-old had graduated and planned to go to Ferrum College.

This hot Thursday afternoon, Lamont was enjoying the thrill of jumping the high bank and soaring into the cooling water with his friends—until, on what would prove to be his last jump, he submerged and never came back up. Rescuers began searching about 4:30 p.m. The old way of divers sweeping the floor of the quarry was replaced by sweeps of an underwater camera. I was working as the incident's public information officer and was assisting a WRAL news crew three hours later when the camera operator spotted the body. Lamont was about sixteen feet down, wedged against a tree. Divers went down to retrieve him. I wouldn't let the news crew video the recovery, but we did use the zoom lens to observe.

Lamont Burt Jr. is buried in the Historic Oakwood Cemetery in Raleigh. He left behind parents, two sisters and a brother.

## Tuesday, May 28, 2019

The quarry jump spot claimed its second diver four years after we lost Lamont Burt.

Seven days after graduating from Eno River Academy, eighteen-year-old Niklaus Brown was enjoying the Eno Quarry. It was hot, extremely hot, more like July than May. Niklaus was to attend UNC-Wilmington in the fall, but right then his summer break was starting. Tragically, it was ending as well. Niklaus was a strong swimmer, working as a lifeguard at the Sportsplex in Hillsborough. He was a member of the academy's swim and baseball teams.

Niklaus jumped off the high bluff and completed a flip but over-rotated and landed in the water awkwardly. He briefly surfaced, then sank. A cellphone call to Orange County 911 at 5:15 p.m. alerted the state park. A park ranger was there within four minutes and rescue began searching at 5:25 p.m., continuing for four hours, into dark. There were crews that first evening from Orange and Durham Counties and North Carolina State Parks. It took two more days of before efforts began to pay off. An underwater drone scan led to an area of interest. It was a rescue diver from Halifax County who found Niklaus's body. He was twenty-five feet deep.

*Between 1993 and 2019, the deep of the Eno Quarry claimed four young men between the ages of seventeen and twenty-one in good health and conditioning. No alcohol or drugs were involved. Most likely overexertion, possibly combined with dehydration, led to hard times for their grieving families.*

# Last Hike on Cox Mountain

## *Sunday, January 1, 2006*

Since 1971, the Eno River Association has led an annual Hike of the New Year on the Eno. Hiking the Eno on January 1 has become a huge local tradition. The fiftieth consecutive hike occurred on January 1, 2020. This annual event was the first of what has become a national trend of first-day hikes on America's state parks. When the year starts out with mild weather, there have been occasions more than eight hundred hikers participated. The hike gathers at two o'clock in the afternoon and usually starts with words of welcome, reports of association successes in protecting the Eno over the past year and looking ahead to more conservation in the upcoming year. The hike ends with popcorn, roasting marshmallows and drinking hot chocolate.

For a long time, the hike has really been two hikes, a long and a short for hikers to choose. State Park rangers sweep both hikes, ensuring no one gets left behind, and they are available for emergencies, which never happen, until this day. This year, the long hike was the nearly four-mile Cox Mountain Trail, starting at the Fews Ford picnic area. Ranger Adrienne Wallace was

The base of Cox Mountain from the river.

sweeping with an association volunteer. Scattered among the long train of hikers are more volunteers with means of communicating issues. We always leave a ranger at the starting point to coordinate logistical and emergency needs. This year it was me, although I always prefer to go on the hike. The Cox Mountain hike departed after the opening greeting, about 2:15 p.m., led by volunteer Cathy Harris. Temperature was just right, fifty-eight degrees, so we had hundreds of hikers. The only damper was a gray overcast sky.

Cox Mountain in my mind is more of a big hill than a mountain, but you do gain three hundred feet in elevation, and it is steep. Back then, the trail was an old jeep road that went straight up, no switchbacks or meandering. It has a broad summit adorned with a beautiful, open oak-hickory forest. Even when it is not the first of January, it is the most popular trail at Eno River State Park and includes the most famous man-made feature on the Eno, a cable suspension footbridge across the river.

As the first hikers neared the top of the mountain, Christopher Horton of Timberlake was impatient with the pace of the hike. Caught in a long line of hikers, he ran around them to the front and ran ahead of Cathy. He was not alone. Other hikers who didn't like the slow pace went ahead. Out in front now and hiking faster, he didn't get far before spotting another hiker who forged ahead, William H. "Bill" Jewett. Only Bill wasn't hiking. He was lying on the trail, and he wasn't responding.

Not sure what to do, Christopher tried to call his mother at home on his cellphone and then called his father, Eddie, elsewhere on the hike. Eddie called 911 but wasn't alone. By this time, several hikers were calling for help. Hike leader Harris was quickly there. She saw Jewett was blue and facedown. Harris used her cellphone to call the volunteer sweep hiking with Ranger Wallace, still on the steep climb up the slope behind all the slow people. It took Wallace four minutes of hard hoofing to reach Bill. The time was 2:57 p.m. Before she arrived, the park's Mobile Radio Telephone Interconnect sounded off. This was a system allowing emergency personnel to call rangers' two-way radios from a telephone. Ranger Wallace answered. It was Orange County 911 Communications reporting a possible cardiac arrest and asking for someone to call them by telephone. I could hear the whole conversation on my radio, and I called them back on the park cellphone. This was our first indication at the hike base that something was wrong. Cellphone reception was poor, but I gathered the incident was on Cox Mountain. Reception was always bad because we had to use whichever cellphone carrier had the state contract, regardless of how poor coverage was in the park.

Wallace radioed as she ran from the back of the line to the front that she thought the incident was on her hike, and I relayed that information to the 911 center. She radioed minutes later the cardiac arrest was on top of Cox Mountain and CPR was in progress. I called the 911 center back on my personal cellphone because it actually had coverage, told them the situation and to have Eno Fire and Rescue meet me at the Piper-Cox House upriver. From the Piper-Cox House, we could drive through the river at Fews Ford and by a combination of abandoned roads, and a transmission powerline, it was possible to drive near the top of the mountain.

I had my park Chevrolet Blazer, and Eno Fire and Rescue arrived in an SUV with Keith Hayes driving. I put one volunteer rescuer in with me for radio communications, and we drove across the river and up the mountain. On the way, Wallace radioed that Bill was sixty yards up the trail from the powerline, toward the summit. It is a mile-and-half drive to the Cox Mountain Trail up near the top of the mountain. The last half mile there is no path, only powerline right-of-way. It requires driving up the steep north slope, rocky and rugged terrain, through brush. Driving through rivers, on bumpy trails and up the side of rugged mountains was not normal for volunteer fire and rescue. But one of the privileges of being a ranger is getting to drive where no one else is allowed. I knew a route that would get us there without getting stuck or rolling over. The line of hikers was waiting on us at the high point of the powerline, where the trail crossed. I led the rescuers to Bill, where they took over CPR from Ranger Wallace and other hikers. Being in a community of world-class hospitals meant there were doctors and nurses on the hike pitching in.

Bill was not breathing and had no pulse. While CPR was in progress, I could see a scar on his chest, possibly from past heart surgery. Meanwhile, back at the Piper-Cox house, two paramedics in Dodge Durangos and Orange Rescue Squad with a John Deere Gator arrived. Keith Hayes directed them to the mountaintop by radio but got concerned they wouldn't find us so he drove back, encountering them halfway down the mountain. The paramedics brought an automatic external defibrillator (AED). They shocked Bill seven times on that mountaintop and got a pulse and blood pressure back. He still wasn't breathing on his own, so artificial respiration continued.

Bill didn't bring anyone along with him on the hike, so there was no one to tell Ranger Wallace who he was. She found his wallet in his pocket and identified him with his driver's license so we then knew who we were trying to save. We placed Bill on a stretcher and loaded the stretcher on Orange

Rescue's Gator, carrying him down the narrow trail to the powerline. There he was transferred into the back of the Eno Rescue SUV with medical care continuing. I led everyone the jostling mile and a half drive back to the other side of the river. While we were en route, the UNC Medical Center helicopter was called and landed in Fowler Field, adjacent to the picnic area. Bill was taken directly there and transferred to the helicopter.

Everyone signs in on Eno River Association hikes with an emergency contact. Association staff were able to give me Bill's home phone number. At 4:20 p.m., more than an hour and a half after Bill collapsed, the helicopter took off for Chapel Hill's UNC medical center. I took one breath and then called his wife, Julia.

I told Julia what happened, where and how Bill had been taken. She told me a few things about Bill, telling me he was sixty-nine but thought he was eighteen. He took medication for his heart, confirming to me this was not a new situation. She told me if he had to go, this is what he would want to be doing. Fortunately, her daughter was in town and could take her to the hospital.

Bill was pronounced dead at UNC Hospital. He had moved to Chapel Hill four months earlier and was just discovering the Eno River. He had retired from a long career as a railroad finance officer and financial planner. He was an active Rotarian. Bill was also a fervent conservationist and served as an officer for an Indiana land trust. A private memorial service was held on January 6 at United Church of Chapel Hill.

# River Spirit

## Friday and Saturday, February 23 and 24, 2007

Ranger Joe Martin and I were working the closing shift. I was closing Occoneechee Mountain State Natural Area. Martin was closing Eno River State Park. Back then, park gates locked at six o'clock in the evening during February. Closing Fews Ford Access, Joe still had a maroon Honda in the picnic area parking lot. I wrapped up Occoneechee and drove back to help him. Usually, we would find overdue park visitors lingering in high-use areas. Joe checked the swinging cable bridge, the wilderness cabin and the Cox Mountain group camp. I searched the Fanny's Ford Campground. Joe ran the license tag, found the owner's name and address and tried to look up the owner's phone number, wanting to call the home to see if we could find out if the driver might be in trouble. When cellular phones became common, we found a lot of people gave up their land lines, making it hard for us to find a contact number. We knew this Honda belonged to Mariam Lee but couldn't find a phone number to call. Park visitors sometimes leave a car in the park intentionally and don't tell rangers, so unless we found at least a snippet of evidence they didn't intend to be there, we would suspend an investigation. This was the case with Mariam's car. At 7:30 p.m. we left a note on her car with instructions in case she returned, and we went off duty. The temperature that night was in the thirties.

Ranger Martin was back on duty Saturday morning. Two neighbors, Ken and Lisa, who lived a short distance outside the Fews Ford gate, were doing an early morning hike on the Eno Trace Trail. They didn't get far when they discovered, on a small footbridge, a complete set of women's clothing, along with jewelry, shoes and underwear, neatly folded. Ken and Lisa knew this wasn't usual and went and found Martin, who called me. Now we had evidence something was very wrong, and our investigation went into high gear. I told him to secure the clothes and drive to the home where the car was registered, a street off Cole Mill Road about four miles from the river access. I set to calling in more rangers.

Martin called me from Mariam's house, where he was with her parents. They told him nineteen-year-old Mariam left work crying at five o'clock yesterday evening and had not come home. While he interviewed the parents for any information to help find her, I set up an incident command at the park office.

You realize how big Eno River State Park is when you want to find one person in it. We needed help, and that help needed to know how to search wilderness effectively and efficiently, a skill few people have. We got resources in from Umstead and Falls Lake State Parks; Orange County Emergency Management, Rescue Squad and Sheriff's Office; Durham Fire Department; three specialized volunteer search and rescue teams; three swift water teams; and the State Bureau of Investigation (SBI). There were seventy-two people looking for Mariam.

Ranger Martin came to the command post with Mariam's stepfather. He brought us the key to the Honda and a picture. She was a beautiful young woman, and we were sincerely hoping nothing happened to her. Her mother came as well but walked away to go out on the trails looking. That is never good, as it deprives the search investigators the opportunity to get useful information and sets up for someone else to get lost or hurt. A good investigation goes a long way toward narrowing down the search area for a missing person. Eno River ranger Christopher Ammon was assigned the search of Mariam's car. He found journal-like writings that seemed to indicate she was upset over a boy. Nothing said she would harm herself, but the writings did give us a clue to her state of mind. We were also able to piece together a timeline from leaving work to when her car was first seen at the park. It was a narrow window without time to pick someone else up. Every indication was she was alone.

Most missing people in the park who are despondent are found on land. I had never had one in the water. It is also true that in similar situations we found most of our missing people alive, and that continued to be the hope. A land search of Fews Ford Access began shortly after noon. Ground crews and dog teams were deployed. Teams searched riverbanks, woods around the Trace Trail, Fowler Field, woods up to the abandoned Hillsborough Coach Road and downriver to a transmission powerline. Both sides of the river were covered.

It was thoroughness that led us to put swift water teams searching the river. The Rescue Extrication and Delivery Specialists (REDS) from Raleigh drove down the old abandoned road to Cabe Ford and worked upriver back toward the Eno Trace Trail. South Orange Rescue Squad began at the swinging bridge and worked downstream. Both had inflatable boats and divers. The boats followed the divers, who checked the river bottom. By midafternoon we had Youngsville Rescue's swift water team ready to work upriver from the swinging bridge.

At 3:25 p.m., South Orange Rescue radioed they found Mariam. She was 220 yards downstream from where her clothes were left, just past where the Eno Trace trail loops away from the river up into the woods. She lay on the bottom, four feet deep. She had likely been in the river since darkness fell the night before. Her spirit had lifted out of the river many hours before we got to her.

Rangers went to secure the scene. My supervisor, District Superintendent Billy Totten, and I went to the Fews Ford picnic area where we knew Mariam's mother was waiting. We broke the news. She was every bit as distraught as you would expect. She wanted to see the body, but we didn't allow that. We didn't want her seeing Mariam until she could be cleaned up. Then I went to the river with SBI agent Denning to investigate.

South Orange Rescue had anchored a boat at the spot, and a diver was in the water. He brought the Mariam up and to the bank on the same side as the Eno Trace Trail. She was nude and had no marks other than

Mariam climbed in the river here along the Eno Trace Trail.

scuffed knees. The speculation was after she drowned, she drifted, with the underwater current, face down and scuffed her knees on rocks. Mariam was pulled out, placed in a yellow body bag and rolled out of the woods on a bicycle wheel stretcher. At the picnic area, she was loaded on an ambulance and taken to the medical examiner in Chapel Hill.

The following day, Sunday, an autopsy determined Mariam died from drowning. There was no evidence of a crime. Tests that took weeks to come back proved there were no drugs or alcohol in her system. Our presumption was suicide. There was never any indication otherwise, but there is no way to be sure. We do know on a cold February night, Mariam carefully took off all her clothing and jewelry and put them neatly on the footbridge. She then waded into the frigid river, on hard rocks, with the cold exaggerating the stinging pain in her feet. Then she held herself underwater until she drowned in depths where she could stand with her head above water. Between her clothes and where she drifted, there is no water deeper than four feet. Or alternatively, she sat in the freezing cold water until hypothermia overtook her. Whichever happened, it took remarkable determination.

Mariam's family donated a unique and beautiful bench in her memory that was installed along the river where her body was found. In those days, we weren't allowed to put names or memorials on donations, but it served those of us who knew its meaning. It stayed in that spot for many years, but because repeated river floods threatened it, a few years ago it was moved to the covered deck of the park office, where it remains today. Please remember a beautiful spirit when you rest on her bench.

# Downriver Drowning

## *Saturday and Sunday, August 14 and 15, 2010*

Where the Eno and Flat Rivers converge to form the Neuse is game lands, owned by the U.S. Army Corps of Engineers and managed by the North Carolina Wildlife Commission. The backwaters of Falls Lake inundate the river for over a mile upstream, making the river deep and slow but no wider. This stretch of the river is popular for boaters and fishermen. It was some fishermen who found Damien Mahaffey on August 14.

We don't know much about Mahaffey. There was precious little press coverage. He was thirty-eight years old and lived nearby in Butner. On Saturday, his mother reported him missing. On Sunday morning, his body was found in the river about seven o'clock in the morning, down near the confluence with the Flat. Durham Sheriff's Office said it looked like natural causes, but they did send him to the medical examiner to confirm.

## 5

# TRAGEDY AVERTED

## An Infant's Cry

### Friday, August 6, 1896

Ed Rogers was a civic leader in the Lebanon Township, on the lower Eno. A year earlier, he had been appointed magistrate, and in a couple of years Ed would be appointed election judge. On this summer day, he was plying his trade, which was tobacco. Ed was curing the golden leaf near Vandergriff's Lumber Yard, just up the hill from the river, near the Lynchburg and Durham Railroad. He was startled to hear a baby crying and, out of concern, began following the sounds.

Inside a shanty at the lumberyard, Ed found a suitcase, and it sounded like the crying was coming from inside. Opening the case, he found a baby girl, about two months old. The baby was well dressed, with a good supply of quality clothing in the suitcase with her. Most importantly, she was alive.

Ed rode to Durham and reported the incident to county officials. He himself saw to the care of the baby. He even employed a woman to serve as a wet nurse. But in the ensuing days, there was no clue as to who abandoned the infant or who was the mother.

The *Durham Sun* newspaper came out on August 25 with some titillating details. According to the *Sun*, facts regarding the mysterious waif were leaking out. They claimed the parents were from an adjoining county. The father was an influential, well-to-do citizen, active in church work and not married to the mother. It was rumored the father gave the young mother money and sent her away. He hired a man to wait on her and assist her with leaving and concealing the child. The woman was rumored to have spent two to three days in Durham, to which there were several witnesses. The man assisting her was also seen in town when he tried to borrow a quarter from a *Durham Sun* reporter. The *Sun* claimed to have the names of all parties in their possession but believed it prudent to withhold the names for now. They could produce the names but were allowing time for authorities to investigate and set up a trial. The newspaper was in the dark regarding the location of the mother and the man helping her but did know where the father lived.

News reports diminish after August, leaving us wondering what became of the innocent in all this, the abandoned baby? Was the mother ever found, and was anyone ever held to account? Did she plan to return? And was the intent to leave the infant in a safe place to be discovered? Or more sinister, was the intent abandoning the baby to perish?

# Durham's Vanished Girl

## Wednesday, June 17, 1942

On a Wednesday night on McMannen Street in Durham, Rebecca Robinson left to go to the movies and then vanished. She was thirteen years old, a student at Central Junior High, five feet, two inches, tall, 110 pounds, brown eyes. Over the next couple months, the newspapers didn't fail to mention how pretty she was. She lived with her mother, Mabel King, who watched her leave in a blue and white polo shirt and a white dress with fruit designs.

As the investigation plowed through June, attention turned to eighteen-year-old Clyde Tilley of Route 4, Durham. Clyde's story was that he and Rebecca drove out to the Eno River on Friday, June 19, to go swimming, two days after leaving home. When they got there, Rebecca refused to go in the water and waited in the car while he went in. After he got out, he lay on the riverbank and fell asleep for a short nap. Waking, he went back to the car and Rebecca was gone. Clyde said he called for and looked along the riverbank for some time. Failing to find her, he went home.

On July 2, fifteen days since her mother last saw her and based on the information they now had from Tilley, Durham Sheriff E.G. "Cat" Belvin and his deputies searched the riverbank but found no traces of Rebecca. Firmly believing that Rebecca had either drowned or met foul play, the sheriff expanded the search into the Eno on July 3. He called on six divers and swimmers from the city recreation department under the supervision of Dick Morris of the Durham Red Cross Lifesaving Corps. Beginning at the place Rebecca was last seen, they spent the day on a thorough check of the river bottom. It was another day of no trace. Mabel King refused to believe her daughter was dead, telling reporters, "I know she is alright. I feel it. I just know she is." Neither the sheriff's department nor Durham City Police were hopeful.

It was July 6, nineteen days gone, when a report came out that Rebecca might have eloped to South Carolina with fifteen-year-old George Caton. George used to live in Rebecca's neighborhood. This line of thought proved erroneous the next day, as George was not missing and found working for Augusta Roofing Company at Camp Butner. He said he had not seen her for two months.

July 9, twenty-two days missing, and Sheriff Belvin no longer believed Rebecca was dead or suffering from nefarious activity. If she had drowned, he was confident the divers would have found her. He now believed she was in another state and definitely not in Durham County. He sent out notices and her description statewide. Over the next few days, the investigation continued.

July 13, twenty-six days passed, Clyde Tilley was out on a $500 bond with a court date of August 12. The charge was having carnal knowledge with Rebecca. He had confessed to having carnal knowledge with the thirteen-year-old on the night before they went to the river. The court date was set based on the expectation Rebecca would be found by then, with the intent to postpone if she was still missing. There were reports she had been seen on Durham streets, but deputies combed the streets thoroughly and Sheriff Belvin stated unequivocally those reports were false. He was of the belief she had left the state and might be in South Carolina.

Then two more teenage Durham girls disappeared. Fifteen-year-old Betty Lou Hicks went missing on July 13. Seventeen-year-old Audrey Brock followed on July 14. County and city officials had no leads, but the search was continuing for all the girls. Telephones were ringing constantly at the Durham newspapers and the sheriff's office, calls coming in from many concerned local citizens.

Two days after Audrey Brock was reported missing, Audrey's stepfather spotted her in a car with a soldier in West Durham. He gave chase, and after considerable argument with the belligerent soldier, he took custody of Audrey and took her home. Acting Durham police chief H.E. King stated he though Rebecca and Betty Lou were probably gone for the same reason as Audrey.

On July 20, with Rebecca gone thirty-three days, Betty Lou returned to Durham claiming she had knowledge of the whereabouts of Rebecca. Rebecca was all right, but Betty Lou was not telling where she was. Betty Lou herself had run off to Dillon, South Carolina, and married an army lieutenant.

August 3, forty-seven days after Rebecca went to the movies, a reporter for the *Durham Sun* was working the Durham County Courthouse. In a nearly empty superior courtroom, he saw a familiar face he knew, from pictures in the newspaper, talking to Chief of Detectives W.E. Burgess. He called out her name, "Rebecca." She turned and admitted her identity. After her conference with the police, Rebecca declined to say where she had been or why she left. We join the citizens of Durham in the summer of '42, left to wonder.

*During the summer of 1942, World War II was raging. There were many young soldiers at Camp Butner in northern Durham County. It is expected they would be looking for romance among the locals.*

# Scared and Voiceless

## Wednesday and Thursday, August 29–30, 1951

Seven-year-old Jesse Martin Jr. lived on the family farm with three younger siblings. Jesse was mute but could hear fine. His father worked on the nearby Watson farm. That farm was on the lower Eno, half a mile from Hamlin Road and several miles north of Catsburg. Wednesday afternoon about four o'clock, Jesse was in Mr. Watson's yard playing when he wandered off.

Neighbors searched for Jesse from late afternoon to midnight, using flashlights. Late in the day, his parents notified the Durham County Sheriff's Office (DCSO). The search on Wednesday was fruitless.

Come Thursday, needing more manpower, the DCSO issued a radio call for Boy Scouts, and about seventy-five responded. The scouts began searching the farm around 2:00 p.m. Fearing the worst, searchers hit the danger spots first, especially along the Eno where in some places the banks dropped twenty feet to the water. (That depth was reported by the newspapers, but it is less than ten feet.) Searchers lined up side by side and swept areas several hundred yards wide with each sweep across farm fields. Airplane pilot Omar Dodson of Durham flew his Piper Cub over the search scene for two hours, covering every open space there was. He landed in a field to coordinate with the search managers and then returned to the air. Before taking off, Dodson expressed his fear that Jesse was in the river.

Jesse had been missing twenty-four hours when tall, gangling David Rogers of Boy Scout Troop 13 spotted the terrified boy on thick grass under a sycamore tree, about a mile from the Watson house. Jesse was only wearing a T-shirt, having lost the diaper his parents said he was wearing when last seen. He was wide awake but too scared and weak to walk. The whole time he was lost he did not eat or drink, not even going down to the river for water. Omar Dodson saw the find from the air and flew to Jesse's house and shouted the good news down. Scout leaders administered first aid and carried Jesse back to his house on an improvised stretcher. He was crying and scared until he saw Mr. Watson, the first person he knew, which made him break out in a grin.

Jesse was checked out at Lincoln Hospital in Durham. His condition was good, and they were able to send him home.

# Perilous Rescue

## Thursday, March 4, 1993

The events of March 4, 1993, really had their beginning 145 years earlier. That's when Squire William Guess built his mill and dammed the Eno River. The dam was necessary to store enough water to operate the mill and to raise the level so water could be let down the millrace to power the waterwheel. The mill was down beside what we now call Guess Road in Durham. The dam was 350 yards farther upriver. It was so far upriver, you couldn't see the mill from the headrace gate at the dam. The person opening the gate would blow a trumpet so the miller would know the water was coming.

A millstone and old chimney mark where the Guess/Geer mill stood. The Laurel Bluffs Trail passes this site.

Squire Guess went bankrupt after the Civil War and sold the mill to Fred Geer. Of the mills taken out by the great flood of 1908, it was the only one rebuilt. The dam was rebuilt or recapped in 1923. It's uncertain when the mill ceased operation. Today the Laurel Bluffs hiking trail passes through the old mill site and the dam, even traveling through the abandoned millrace. At the mill site, a chimney stands and old corn grinding stones lie on the ground. Continue upriver and there is a great view of the dam from the trail. Two-thirds of the dam is there, but the end on river right is gone. This is because the last owner of the mill, Dr. George Johnson, dynamited the dam out of fear someone would drown in the millpond. Based on Eno River history, he was probably right. The opening in the dam makes a great drop in the river that is fun for kayaks and canoes. This is important to what happened in 1993.

Starting Wednesday night, March 3, and into Thursday morning, March 4, it rained heavy; three and a half inches came down fast and hard. This meant there was a lot of runoff, which is the recipe for fast-rising streams. Apartment complexes in Chapel Hill flooded. Parks and roads in Durham were underwater. The Eno rose nine feet, straight up.

Thursday was a cool day, fifty-five degrees with light rain, and it was windy. That afternoon, two nineteen-year-olds, Derrick Wilson and Philip Smith, went to Durham's premier outdoor store, River Runners Emporium, and rented a canoe. They told store manager Carl Malatin they were going to Lake Michie fishing, knowing all along that was not their intent. Carl warned them that local rivers were treacherous and to stay off them. Phillip and Derrick assured him they would follow his advice.

Instead, they drove straight to the Cole Mill Road bridge, which crosses the river within Eno River State Park. They put the boat on the river about 1:50 p.m. and took off in the swift-moving water. The canoe they rented was a lake style, not meant for moving water. At least they were wearing life jackets. Three miles downriver, the Guess/Geer Dam waited.

The stone-and-concrete Guess/Geer dam is usually eight feet above the river with all the water pushing right passing around the broken end. On this day, the river wasn't going around the dam, high water was passing right over the top of the dam and then dropping as a thundering waterfall into a churning hydraulic. Hydraulics occur when a lot of fast-moving water makes a sudden drop, and the river circulates in a powerful spinning and turbulent current going down the bottom, circling to the top, then back down again, trapping anything that falls into it in a perpetual rotation. They are a deadly hazard to boaters.

What is usually a leisurely float from Cole Mill to the dam took Derrick and Philip only twenty minutes. The river was racing. Just above the dam, they pulled over, stopped and asked a man walking along the river (a resident of Open Air Camp Road) if he thought they could "shoot the dam." He told them it was their risk. Later, in retrospect, he said he probably should have told them, "No," but was trying not to treat them like kids.

Pushing off the bank, the canoe approached the dam. Things swiftly turned to chaos. The canoe turned sideways less than ten feet from the dam and struck a tree. Philip and Derrick were thrown out. The canoe was sucked over the dam and under the hydraulic, not to be seen again. Growing out of crack in the top of that old stone dam was a spindly tree, about six inches in diameter. As the river washed the canoeists to the top of the dam, they clung to that tree, scrambled up the trunk and onto the crook of some branches, staring down into the roaring waterfall below. There they were, perched about six feet up that tree.

Derrick and Philip screamed for help until an area resident heard them and called 911. Rescue teams arrived, followed by crowds of onlookers and news reporters.

On March 4, 1993, the river was flowing over this dam, not around it.

I was new to the Eno River State Park, having been a ranger there barely a month. I had not even seen the Guess/Geer Dam when we got the call, and here is how we got the call. Back in those days, the state park did not have radio communications with local emergency services. The Eno River Association owned and rented out, as a residence, the old Open Air Camp Lodge, which was on the bluff above the dam. Paul Benzing, who rented the lodge, called the executive vice president of the association, Margaret Nygard. Nygard called the state parks district superintendent (and former Eno River State Park superintendent) Susan Tillotson at her office in Raleigh. At 3:15 p.m., Tillotson called me on the state parks' two-way radio. I can't remember where on the Eno we were, but it took twenty minutes for Ranger Scott Hartley to arrive and another twenty-five minutes before I got there. We came in on Open Air Camp Road, the north bank.

At the request of the incident commander, Scott and I flagged a line to keep spectators and media back and carried equipment and guided rescue personnel to the opposite bank. This meant hiking through forest and brush from Guess Road. There was no Laurel Bluffs Trail in those days, and if there had been, it would have been under deep water. The river, normally about one hundred feet wide and running clear, was more than doubled in width and a frothy chocolate-milk brown. Normally a person can walk right off the riverbank onto the top of the dam. On this day, the river completely covered the dam and stretched up the steep bluff above it. The tree protecting Derrick and Philip was sixty feet from land. The river was so loud and the canoeists so far out, rescuers had to use a bullhorn to shout instructions to them. It was too far to throw a rope, and there were too many tree branches in the way.

The Rescue Extrication Delivery Specialists team from Raleigh went to work trying to set up a tricky high angle rescue up in tall trees. Downstream from the dam the Durham County Sheriff's Office divers successfully set a safety line across the river. The thought was if Derrick or Philip fell out of the tree and managed to escape the hydraulic, they could grab the rope as they washed downstream.

At the bottom of the dam, the hydraulic was lethal. I watched as large logs washed over the dam and spun relentlessly, like they were trapped in a giant washing machine. Running out of safe options, Durham Emergency Management reached out to the state Emergency Management. The state contacted the Fifty-Seventh Medical Company out of Fort Bragg, who arranged for a Black Hawk helicopter.

Pilot Robert Beatty later said it was unusual for them to do civilian rescues. His crew recognized Beatty as a pilot extraordinaire, a phenomenal aviator. They had faith in him every time they lifted off. With him that day were co-pilot Dave Mynott, operations crew chief Fred Halverson and medic Eric Kessinger. The assigned crew that day were enormously qualified for rescue, with one exception. This operation was going to require lowering a rescuer through the trees on a jungle penetrator seat, and no one on the crew was trained to be the one dangling at the end of the cable. It just so happened the Medic Jeff Hewitt came on to the base that afternoon to prepare a training class he was to lead that night. Hewitt was not only qualified to ride the penetrator, but he also taught others how to do it, so he was recruited into the rescue. The rescue request went in at 3:30 p.m., but with administrative processes, getting the bird ready and travel time, it was 5:30 p.m. before it was hovering over the river. An hour and a half of daylight was left.

The big chopper hovered sixty feet above the river. Prop wash was throwing wet leaves, sticks and water all around us. Everyone was taking cover behind big trees, which were rocking from the wind. In the crowd, watching from the back was Marsha Poe, Derrick's mother. Her comment as the drama unfolded: "I don't know what they were doing out there, you can't tell them everything." Philip's mother found out when a live shot of the rescue came across the news on her television.

The two teens tightly gripped their tree. The plan was to lower Staff Sergeant Jeff Hewitt on the yellow penetration seat, tethered by cable and winch to the helicopter. The seat has three feet that fold down. Hewitt would be sitting on two of the feet and would pull the victims one at a time onto the third. For extra safety, they added an orange flotation device to the apparatus.

The first try went poorly. The helicopter wasn't positioned right, and hand signal communications weren't working well. Tree branches prevented a frustrated Sergeant Hewitt from getting close. Halverson winched Hewitt back up. Beatty repositioned the helicopter, and they tried again. The penetrator seat punched through the tree limbs. Hewitt was close but not quite there. Hewitt yelled at the men not to jump on and waved his hands, signaling for them to stay on the tree. He didn't know if the cable could withstand the sudden shock of a full-grown man landing on the seat. There was also the danger of a jolt of static electricity if they grabbed the cable, which could knock them out of the tree. Hewitt grabbed a branch to discharge the electricity. Now everything was ready.

Derrick gripped the tree with one hand, leaned and reached out with the other, grasping the sergeant's outstretched hand and pulled him over to the tree. Now things were happening. Hewitt put a harness on Derrick, and the two were winched through the branches and into the helicopter. Back in the chopper, Hewitt got on internal communications and gave Pilot Beatty instructions on where they needed to be. Beatty adjusted their position over the trees, and the operation was repeated to rescue Philip. This time, the seat penetrated perfectly. Both canoeists were on the helicopter twenty-three minutes after it arrived, more than three and a half hours after climbing up that tree. The last thing Sergeant Hewitt did was wave at the Durham Sheriff's Dive Team below. Until he was hoisted up with Philip, he hadn't realized there were rescuers in the water waiting to catch them if they fell into the river.

They were flown to a nearby field, where a crowd gathered to welcome the men and the flight crew. The landing became somewhat of a celebration. Derrick's mom, Marsha, made a point of thanking Sergeant Hewitt, something that doesn't actually happen much in rescue operations. Another woman, hearing Hewitt was thirsty after a couple hours in the air, got him a juice box out of her car. Philip and Derrick were loaded into ambulances and driven to Duke Hospital to be evaluated for exposure. Hewitt made it back to Fort Bragg in time to lead his night class, and the whole crew got thank-you letters from the families in subsequent weeks.

That was Thursday. On Saturday, I was in my patrol car in the park and encountered our maintenance chief Floyd Barbour driving out of the Cole Mill Access in his park truck. As guys are want to do, we rolled down the windows and had a conversation in the road. Floyd had one of our community service workers with him, a court-ordered volunteer working off a cocaine possession sentence. Floyd said he heard we had some excitement. I said, "Yeah, these two fools tried to canoe the river when the water was up Thursday and had to be rescued by helicopter!" Floyd allowed he knew all about it, because one of those fools was sitting beside him, our community service worker. That young man told us when he was up in that tree and the helicopter was having trouble reaching them, he considered jumping from the tree, certain he could clear the hydraulic. I was there—I saw he would not.

*To see an on-location video presentation of this event, with photography from the rescue, see the video at https://www.youtube.com/watch?v=_lFDy7u0cNE.*

# Dark Night on Moore Creek

## *Tuesday and Wednesday, March 26 and 27, 1996*

*Family names are changed at their request for privacy. All other persons, places and events are factual as occurred.*

It was getting dark, and I was on patrol doing the closing routine of the Fews Ford Access at Eno River State Park. In those days, we closed the gates at seven o'clock in March. I was going down to check the small Fowler Field parking lot for cars. It wasn't common for anyone to use that lot, but a few people did. This time was unusual. There was a car but not in the lot. It was parked on the shoulder of the gravel road opposite the lot.

The car was a red Ford Taurus. On one side of the road was the large Fowler Field with tall grass, brush and scattered cedar trees. Beyond the field was woods and then the river. On the other side of the road there was lots of forest, leading down and beyond Moore Creek, a pretty and stony tributary of the Eno. If you continue down the one-lane gravel road that takes you past the parking lot, you came upon the old nineteenth-century Shields' house, which the park used for storage, and also the park's tractor

Moore Creek.

shed. From there the road turns to dirt and goes down through woods to a transmission powerline and on to a river bend.

I finished checking Fews Ford for cars, locked the gate and returned to the Taurus. Looking for the driver, I rode down to the tractor shed and on down to the power line, even a side trip to a spot down the hill where we dumped wood, stumps and other debris. As I drove in the early darkness, I shone a spotlight through open areas and called out. Obviously, none of this worked or there would not be a story to tell. I inspected the car from the outside, looking for clues, and then ran the license tag through Orange County communications.

The car belonged to Nora Irvin of Durham. I looked up her phone number, and luckily she answered. I told her who I was and asked if she knew why her car was there after closing hours. Nora told me the car was driven by her husband, Chris, and he was suicidal. She had notified Durham Police and the Highway Patrol to watch for him. I told her she needed to come out to the park and talk to me immediately. She gave me a description of Chris, and I assured her we would begin searching for him.

So, who was Chris Irvin? Chris came to Durham more than thirty years before to study psychology at Duke University. He stayed and had a stellar career as a psychologist. He worked with hospital patients. He taught classes in child development. He directed outpatient mental health clinics, conducted group and individual psychotherapy and did mental evaluations for disability determination. He managed a crisis and suicide program and worked with patients on alcohol rehabilitation. For years, he taught graduate and undergraduate university courses. Chris did a lot for caring for the mental health of the people of Durham. He was prominent in his field and had a personal life, too. He loved his family, tennis, writing and his church. But Chris was not immune to the demons of mental illness. Now sixty-four years old, after a career helping others, he needed help. Some voice in his head was telling him he had to die, and he came to the Eno River to do it. We had to find him, return him to those who loved him and get him the help he had so long provided others.

The evening temperatures started in the low fifties. By early morning, we were in the low forties. Alone in the office, I began calling in trained search and rescue resources. Durham Search and Rescue was first on my list. I knew this group well. I had joined their team three years earlier, and we went all over the state looking for people lost in the wilderness. I asked them to send search crews, dog teams and search incident managers. I called Orange County Sheriff's Office for investigative and additional law enforcement support. Eno River rangers Kevan Burnett and Lori Marlow were called back on duty. I radioed the Falls Lake Rangers requesting search crews.

The first people to arrive were Nora Irvin, Chris's daughter Amelia and son Thomas. This is always tough in a search, when the family is there before you have help. The family is anxious, and you want to give them reassurance. You also need them for critical information. At the same time, there is a lot that needs to be done to prepare for the arriving search and rescue resources so they can be deployed quickly when they arrive. I caught the family up on what I had done so far and had them wait in the park office. When Lieutenant Thomas from the sheriff's department arrived, he took on filling out a lost person questionnaire with the family, which gives search planners information key to leading us to our missing person. During his investigation, we learned Chris was not familiar with the park. Also, he had attempted suicide before by cutting his wrists, and the family feared he would try again.

Durham Search and Rescue arrived at 10:30 p.m. I immediately sent a dog team out to start from the Taurus. Nora Irvin unlocked the Taurus for them so they could collect scent articles and look for clues. They found a receipt from an Alcoholic Beverage Control store from 10:20 that morning. Meanwhile, we were setting up an incident command post at the park office. Rangers from Eno River, Falls Lake and the state parks district office arrived. A ranger was assigned to watch the Taurus in case Chris returned to it. Another ranger patrolled Pleasant Green and Cole Mill Roads in case he came out of the woods. Ranger Fleming did a house-to-house notification on Cabe Ford Road, the closest neighborhood through the woods. Our search and rescue management computer program was fired up. I also put in a request for a helicopter with forward-looking infrared detection capability (heat seeking).

Orange County sent an EMS unit to stay on scene, and Fire Marshal Mike Tapp took charge of logistics. Park neighbors on Cole Mill Road, seeing the string of emergency vehicles, brought snacks, drinks and coffee before they even knew we were looking for a missing person. At 11:30 p.m., Bill Gentry from North Carolina Emergency Management arrived. A Red Cross food unit was there at midnight to support the searchers. It was during this late-night period we learned another important piece of information. I called the Eno River State Park maintenance chief Louis Delozier. He told me he saw that Taurus arrive between ten and eleven o'clock that morning. We now knew some key things. Chris Irvin had purchased alcohol right before coming in the park and probably had it with him, which is always dangerous in the wilderness. Also, he had been unaccounted for in the park more than twelve hours, which raised the concern that he was in serious trouble and elevated the urgency of our search.

We had thirty-nine people out there that night, searching or supporting the searchers. We received a tip from Cabe Ford Road that someone had seen a person enter a crawl space under a house. Rangers Burnette and Marlow crawled through that space at eleven o'clock at night. Six search crews, three including trained search dogs, took to the field covering assigned areas and routes. When people are despondent, it is common for them to seek areas of natural beauty, so we especially concentrated on the river. Most of the crews returned between 1:00 a.m. and 2:30 a.m. The searchers from Durham Search and Rescue were well-trained volunteers, but they also had jobs to be at in the morning, and we released those who needed to go as they wrapped up their missions.

At 1:15 a.m. we had a planning meeting with the Durham Search and Rescue managers, state parks leadership, county and state emergency managers. Plans were made for continuing operations and new efforts in the morning. We determined we had enough rangers to initiate one more search mission this night. At 1:50 a.m., Search Crew 4 began working the woods between the Ford Taurus and Moore Creek. Before that we had concentrated in the opposite direction toward the river. On the crew were my supervisor, North District superintendent Susan Tillotson, Eno River ranger Kevan Burnette and Falls Lake superintendent Tom Jackson.

While Crew 4 was searching, we were writing missions for the next morning, updating maps and computer probability functions and requesting resources for the morning operations. We had trained search and rescue teams from Randolph, Guilford and Wake Counties coming, along with park rangers from Jordan and Kerr Lakes. Then at 2:45 a.m., Crew 4 found Chris.

He was right at five hundred yards south of his car in a forested area. He didn't respond to voice or touch. He was shivering, eyelids slightly open. Respiration was slow and labored. He was cold to touch and had a strong smell of alcohol. He did move slightly. There was no blood, but the crew found two steel knives lying beside him. Chris never got as far as cutting himself. Alcohol, combined with his medications, exacerbated by cold, was killing him. His breathing was deteriorating, and he needed advanced medical care immediately.

I could hear the stress in Superintendent Tillotson's voice when she radioed for EMS and transport. I asked for their location, and then there was silence. The way you report locations in the wilderness is through grid coordinates read off a map. As the lead search and rescue instructor for state parks, I had trained two of these rangers in grid coordinate systems and the other was in the class when I learned them. But if you don't practice those skills, you lose them. In the stress of the moment, as they rendered aid to Chris, none of the three could remember how to read the coordinates. But that was a discussion for the post incident evaluation. Fortunately, Tillotson and Burnette knew the park intimately, and they were only a couple hundred yards from the historic Shields' house. Burnette met the EMS crew there and led them to Chris. We were lucky EMS was staged at the scene, as he was receiving care in minutes. Available searchers were sent into the woods to carry him out on a Stokes basket, where he was loaded into the ambulance and transported to Durham Regional Hospital.

Chris Irvin remained unconscious for another day from the mixture of alcohol and medication. Three days after he awoke, doctors reported him physically recovered but still requiring psychiatric care. He did recover. A few months after this incident, a state parks employee, who was Chris's neighbor, told me she saw him out doing yard work and he was doing well. Chris Irvin lived another thirteen years to the age of seventy-seven, and when he passed, he was laid to rest at the church he loved.

When daylight arrived, I went out to the spot where Chris was found. It was easy to track the EMS crew and searchers through the woods. At the site I found a liquor bottle and his glasses. It was a lovely spot, beautiful woods looking down on Moore Creek. I understood why Chris chose it. I'm just glad we got there in time, so it wasn't the last beautiful place he saw.

*I looked for a lot of lost people in my career. Rarely did anyone come back after the fact and thank us for finding them or their loved one. This was one of those rare times. The family wrote a gracious thank-you note and made a donation to state parks that we used to buy search and rescue training supplies for rangers.*

# You Don't Know This River

## Thursday and Friday, September 5 and 6, 1996

The Eno River is normally quiet and shallow as it weaves between a galaxy of rocks. Sudden rainstorms can turn it into a chaotic torrent, angry and powerful. Its drop in elevation (fall) corresponds with great speed in the flow. The river rises swiftly with run off and drains back down to safe levels quickly.

Hurricane Fran came on the heels of three days of rain, blowing across the Eno River Valley the night of September 5 and continuing into the early morning hours of September 6. Sustained winds of forty miles per hour, with gusts higher, knocked down trees all over the valley, taking out all electrical power and burying roads. By three o'clock in the morning, five inches of additional rain had dropped in thirteen hours. The eye of the storm passed over the Eno at 4:30 a.m.

By daylight Friday morning, the storm had passed. The river was rising and racing as the creeks flushed in. In Durham, the Old Farm neighborhood had to be evacuated, as the lower Eno, normally one hundred feet wide, became four hundred yards wide. Everywhere the river was well up into the surrounding forest. The shallow Eno crested at twenty-two feet.

The Eno River community was in survival mode. People were stuck at home trying to deal with damage and lack of utilities. That included all the Eno River State Park rangers, except one. That would be me. I lived in the ranger residence across from the park office at Fews Ford. Recognizing this as a once-in-a-lifetime event, I went out to see, document and photograph the river.

At the Fews Ford Access, the river was just twenty yards from the Piper-Cox House parking lot. Water was four feet deep inside the wilderness cabin. Buckquarter Creek Trail was nearly six feet under. The swinging bridge on the Cox Mountain Trail, normally thirteen to fourteen feet over the river, was under five feet, seven inches of fast-flowing, chocolate milk–brown water. The only way I could look at it was from the bluff above. I couldn't see the far side of the bridge because the crowns of three large fallen trees lay across that end. The river and the trees were putting enormous pressure on the bridge. I could not see underneath the river surface, where the six-by-six timber supports on the far landing had snapped like toothpicks. The only reason the landing didn't float away was because the steel cables held.

The swinging bridge in Eno River State Park.

Some 95 percent of the Pleasant Green Access was underwater. At the Pleasant Green Road Bridge, the river rose twenty feet straight up, five feet from topping the road. After the river receded, I saw boulders as big as cars had been moved along the Holden Mill Trail.

Later that afternoon, I was walking between my house and the park office. The park gate was shut and locked. My sons Scott, seven, and Grey, five, were with me. We saw two men carrying a canoe down from the gate toward us. With all the trees and powerlines down on the roads, I don't know how they drove there. I stopped them and explained to them who I was and how dangerous the river was. They told me it was OK: "We know this river." I told them, "You don't know this river. No one has ever seen this river before."

They were insistent. There is no law against stupid. So, I had each write down the contact information for their next of kin, and they went on their way down the hill to Fews Ford to launch. I was still outside eight minutes later when I heard them screaming for help.

I ran down to the ford. Because the river was well up into the forest, all I could do was follow the edge of the water downstream through the trees. I watched and yelled for the canoeists, fearing the worst. It is four-tenths of a mile from the ford to the swinging bridge. By this time, it had been hours since I checked the bridge, and the river had dropped some. Now there were only a few inches of water flowing over the tread. I could also get down close to the landing on my side. But I still couldn't see the other end because of the trees piled on it. I was standing there trying to figure out what to do when those two men came wiggling out of the branches and onto the bridge. They were able to walk in the shallow water on the tread back to my side.

They told me they didn't know what happened. They launched and were moving fast. They came up on a tree trunk laying across the river. The river was moving so fast they couldn't stop and the river sucked their canoe under the tree and they didn't see it again. They managed to grab the tree and get to the far shore, where they walked downstream to the bridge.

The river drops so fast that the next day it was back to safe canoeing levels. We got a call from 911 communications warning us of some canoeists getting on the river. I told them not to worry.

*On September 6, when the river was at its highest. I recorded four high-water marks at the Fews Ford and Pleasant Green Accesses. Each of those has a commemorative sign so visitors can appreciate how remarkable it was.*

# A Faint Cry

## *November 10, 2001*

*The name of the missing person has been changed to protect her privacy. All other names, events and locations are as they occurred.*

Back in 2001, the November closing time for the Cole Mill Access of Eno River State Park was 5:30 p.m. Ranger Adrienne Wallace was on duty, closing the four gated accesses to the park. It was getting dark as she arrived at Cole Mill. The parking lots were deserted except two cars, a white Saturn sedan at the lower parking lot near the picnic area and another car green in color, which has no other bearing on this story. She recognized the Saturn from when she patrolled the park an hour earlier. Looking in the front windshield, Wallace didn't see anyone, so she did what we always did, as it was common for hikers to be late getting back. She put a form note on the windshields giving the combination to the lock on the gate to let themselves

As Patricia was hidden behind this tree, her rescuers passed within feet of her.

out, a warning to not repeat staying in the park after closing hours and a promise of returning to check on the cars. Then she left to finish locking buildings and gates at Fews Ford.

As promised, Wallace returned about 6:30 p.m. Now it was really dark. Typical for a November evening, temperatures were in the fifties. The sky was clear, and the stars were out. One car remained: the white Saturn, with no one around. She illuminated the lonely sedan with headlights and flashing emergency lights. A rear window was partially lowered, and that is where Wallace went. This time, she got out her flashlight did a thorough check of the car. In the back seat was blood, a lot of blood, on the seat behind the driver side and pooled on the floorboard. A bloody knife lay on the seat with its hilt on the seat and the six-inch blade suspended above the floor. A crumpled quilt lay among the pool of blood. When she looked outside the door, there were blood drops on the pavement. Still, no one around. Something bad had happened here.

All alone, Wallace had a lot to consider. There could be someone nearby who needed immediate medical help. There could be someone steps away in the woods, violent and dangerous. She was well armed and well trained, but she was alone and couldn't watch everywhere. Wallace was the only ranger on duty within ten miles, which is common on the Eno. There are not enough rangers. She had to be quick about getting backup and reached out to the Durham Police Department. She called Eno ranger Mark Miller, who had closed Occoneechee Mountain that evening and gone off duty. And she called rangers at Falls Lake to find me. I was a scoutmaster in those days and was camping at Falls Lake with my troop. Once they tracked me down, it took only about half an hour to drive from the lake to the Eno. I got there about five minutes to eight.

Wallace, Miller and four police officers were in the Cole Mill parking lot. They had run the license tag and knew the car belonged to a thirty-three-year-old Carrboro woman named Patricia. The police officers brought a search dog, a German shepherd. They scented the dog off the blood trail on the pavement, and it took off with three officers and Ranger Wallace following. Wallace knew her way around the backcountry of the park well, and her job was to communicate their location if they found Patricia and ensure the officers did not lose track of where they were in the night woods. The dog ran straight into the woods behind the parked car and kept going. It went a mile, almost to the Bobbitt Hole, before it lost interest.

Meanwhile, back at the parking lot, I assigned Ranger Miller and the remaining officer to stay with the car. I went north to the park office, two miles away, to set up an incident command post and call in more search resources.

It was around nine o'clock, and all was quiet in the parking lot. The dog team was still far away when Miller and the officer thought they heard a faint cry for help. It was so faint they were trying to convince themselves that they really heard it. Then it came again. They weren't sure if it was even a person, but it sounded like it was in the woods right behind the car.

Uncertain, they walked into the woods, shining their flashlights all around. Not ten feet behind the car was a huge oak tree with a wide trunk. Easing through the brush and around the oak, they shined their lights on Patricia, who was sitting with her back propped against the back side of the tree. The dog had run right past her, and the officers following couldn't see her through the tree and didn't look backward as they kept up with the canine, so they went past her as well. I have known search dogs to find people under remarkably difficult conditions. I have also known the same dogs to go right past their subject. We don't ever really know what is going on in the dog's head, but they are great assets in finding people, so don't let one miss color their value.

Patricia was conscious, but just barely. Her clothes were soaked in blood, and her wrists bore the evidence of the knife. EMS was called and was there quick. Patricia was not a suicidal person, but she had slit her own wrists in the back seat of that car, and then when she didn't die immediately, she walked back in the woods. She sat down behind the tree and passed out. When she woke up, she started crying for help. It seems Patricia had surgery earlier in the day and was under the influence of pain medication. The medication so distorted her thoughts they led her to a dark place in her mind and nearly her demise in a dark place on the Eno. EMS carried her swiftly to the hospital, where in the appropriate time, she recovered.

I notified all the searchers en route to turn around. We cleared the scene at ten o'clock, and I returned to my Scout troop back at Falls Lake.

## 6
# WAR COMES TO THE ENO

## The Hanging of James Few
### *Thursday, May 16, 1771*

In the fall of 1758, William Few Sr. and his family settled on 640 acres on the banks of the Eno, land now encompassed by Eno River State Park. In 1759, they bought an additional two acres at a river crossing and established saw and gristmills. Earthworks from the mills are still present on the Fanny's Ford hiking trail. The mills were good business, but four years later, wanting to prosper, Few moved his family to a plantation on the Eno just east of Hillsborough, where the current Ayr Mount historic site stands today. Here they would operate a tavern for people traveling the old Indian Trading Path, now known as Saint Mary's Road.

These were stormy times in Hillsborough. North Carolinians, although loyal British citizens, were upset with both the type and abusive manner of law enforcement and with dishonest sheriffs. Government fees were perceived as excessive. Records were being falsified. There was collusion between government officials and creditors. Taxation systems were unfair, and tax embezzlement was standard operating procedure. The Regulator movement began to coalesce. Regulators stood for honest government and just administration of the law. Their numbers grew to thousands. The first local protests began in 1766, just three years after the Fews moved close to town. William's son James was swept up enthusiastically in the movement.

Memorial to the hanged Regulators.

There were rumors about why James became a zealot. One story was he was fueled by Edmund Fanning's seduction of his intended bride. Fanning, of Hillsborough, held many government positions. Another story labeled James as a fanatic with prophetic visions of himself as a deliverer from tyranny.

Discouraged over failing to secure justice through peaceful negotiations, the Regulators took a radical stance. Violence, lawlessness and terrorism reigned in the territory. When the government retaliated against them, the Regulators defiantly refused to pay levied fees, terrorizing anyone administering the law and disrupting court proceedings. The Regulators escalated, and government officials dug in their heels. It was leading to a crescendo of confrontation. In 1770, Hillsborough broke out into riot. The despised Edmund Fanning was caught in his home and dragged by his feet down the stairs with his head banging on the steps. Then his home was destroyed. Judge Richard Henderson was harassed until he fled. The home of another government official was raided and all his possessions thrown out on the lawn.

From the colonial capital of New Bern, Governor William Tryon and his council responded with tougher rioting laws. One of the new regulations required citizens to answer a court summons within sixty days, later to be used against James Few. Tryon was being urged to bring in the military to restore order, and in May 1771, he responded, leading troops of the king's militia to the western frontier. After a stop to resupply and rest in Hillsborough, they departed on May 11 to set up on Alamance Creek, now the Alamance Battleground State Historic Site. Five days later, one thousand trained soldiers met up against two thousand Regulators.

Tryon gave the Regulators a choice: return peacefully home or be fired on, and he gave them one hour to decide. At the end of the hour, Tryon sent an officer for their answer, which was, "Fire and be damned!" The governor gave the order to fire, but his men hesitated. Rising in his stirrups, he shouted, "Fire! Fire on them or on me!" Now the militia obeyed, and the Regulators fired back. The Battle of Alamance Creek was on, for a little while.

When the shooting started, many Regulators fled, leaving their bolder compatriots to carry on the fight. Those left behind were no match, and the rebellion was crushed in two hours. Nine members of the king's militia were killed and sixty-one wounded. Nine regulators also died, and many more injured, but there was no count taken. Prisoners were taken by Tryon's forces to face military tribunal, except for one Regulator, who was executed without trial the very next day there in Tryon's encampment on Alamance Creek. That one was James Few. There is no official record as to why James was summarily hanged, but there are rumors. One story was it was done under the pretext as punishment for failing to answer a court summons within the required sixty days. Another story was Few refused to sign the oath of allegiance to the Crown required of Regulators as a condition of pardon. But it was also rumored that he was hanged because he gave the British militia such a fit during the battle that Tryon had him executed to appease his angry soldiers. There may be credence to this last story, as twelve of fourteen other captives taken to Hillsborough were tried and sentenced to death after being convicted of treason. Governor Tryon was reluctant to follow through on the hangings, but to appease his angry soldiers, he hanged six of them to death in Hillsborough on June 19. The other six condemned were pardoned by the king.

James Few was dead, leaving behind his wife, Sally, and three-month-old twins. But Governor Tryon was not through with the Fews. The militia marched back to Hillsborough days after the battle and camped on the Fews' plantation along the Eno. Here they wandered in the planted fields, ruining the crops and, under Tryon's orders, turned the livestock loose. Like many Regulator leaders, the Fews migrated from North Carolina, in their case moving to Georgia. Sally and the twins stayed behind for another ten years until she remarried and at which time James's brother Benjamin fetched the two ten-year-olds to rear in Georgia. James's other brother William Few Jr. rose to prominence in Georgia politics and in 1787 was a signer of the United States constitution. Even in death, James Few was not done with North Carolina. James's great-grandson, also a William, became the first president of Duke University 130 years after James's hanging.

*The hanging of regulators Merrill, Messer, Matter, Pugh and two unknowns took place about 450 yards up the hill from the Eno and less than half a mile west of the Fews' riverfront property. There is a memorial marker on the spot in Hillsborough, behind and up the hill from the Orange County Board of Education building, open to the public for viewing.*

# The Vengeance of Mr. Faddis

## 1776–1801

A certain Mr. Faddis called Hillsborough home during the Revolutionary War. Faddis was an ardent Patriot and soldier for the Continental army. During the war, he had the misfortune of being captured by a band of Tories. The Tories hanged him from a tree limb using a grapevine for a rope and departed, leaving him swinging at his leisure until breath took leave of him. Nearly as soon as the would-be assassins exited, a group of Patriots arrived, found and rescued Faddis. He soon recuperated from his ordeal and was restored to good health.

Twenty years after the war ended, Faddis had long since traded soldier life for that of a tavern keeper in Hillsborough. One fine day he was sitting on the tavern porch and saw a traveler approaching on horseback. The traveler came closer, and closer and closer. Then Faddis recognized him. It was the Tory who "hung him and left him to die a dog's death."

Faddis was a man of violent passions. Generally, this vented in the form of noisy weeping. As soon as he recognized his attempted murderer, he began to blubber and ran into his house for his gun. His wife and other family heard the ruckus and ran to him as he was about to head out the door. Realizing Faddis's highly agitated state, they desperately asked what was the matter?

In between the weeping, Faddis replied in a string of language not fit for polite company that he was going to shoot the Tory who hanged him during the war. This created a loud and vocal stir among the family, and as it grew louder, the neighbors flocked over. With great effort, the neighbors disarmed Faddis and persuaded him to a compromise, to be carried out immediately.

To satisfy Faddis and prevent a murder, the elderly Tory was, with quick deliberation, dismounted and taken to the Eno River. At the river, the crowd enthusiastically dunked him within an inch of his life. Placing the Tory back on his horse, the patriotic Hillsborough citizens warned him if he ever showed up in Hillsborough again, he would receive the fate he tried to carry out on Faddis twenty years earlier. The Tory accepted the terms, never returning to visit Hillsborough or renew his acquaintance with Faddis.

*This account of Mr. Faddis came from the* Petersburg Register *in 1863, reprinted in the* Charlotte Democrat. *The author of the report was not identified but stated he was a Hillsborough native and knew Mr. Faddis, who died of old age when the author was sixteen to seventeen years old. He saw Mr. Faddis frequently, although Faddis was old and decrepit by then.*

# Edenton Bell Battery Cannons

## *1865–1890s*

To understand how the cannons came to be found in the Eno, you have to go back to 1862.

In response to a call from General Beauregard of the Confederate army for cannon making metal, Captain William Badham sent his lieutenant to Edenton, North Carolina, to secure church bells. This was Badham's hometown. All Edenton's churches except the Baptists contributed their bells. Several members of the Baptist Church objected, though whether objecting to the war or loss of the bells is lost in time. Besides the churches, bells were contributed by the town, courthouse, academy and two shipyards. The bells were transported to Tredegar Iron Works in Richmond and cast into four cannons.

Taking command of the cannons, the company commanded by Captain Badham and largely complemented of men from Edenton became known as the Edenton Bell Battery Company. They saw a lot of action in the eastern halves of Virginia and North Carolina. Then, just as the war was coming to an end, Badham feared the cannons would be captured by General Sherman's army. They were on a train passing through Hillsborough. As the train crossed the trestle over the Eno River down from the Hillsborough Depot, the company secretly pushed the cannons out the train car and into the river.

The cannons lay on the river bottom for nearly thirty years until discovered by some Duke students. They managed to get the cannons from their watery storage and swabbed them out. They loaded them to the neck with black powder and gave them a shot for old times' sake. The powder charge was so heavy the cannons exploded all to heck. Several of the adventurers were injured. They were lucky no one died. For decades after the Civil War, there were reports of people trying out old cannons, cannons exploding and fatal results.

*I apologize to the reader. I had an article contemporary with the explosion of the cannons that gave the details of who, where and exactly when, but I lost that article. I had that article before I even found records of where the cannons came from. Somehow it got lost, and I spent an inordinate amount of time trying to relocate that article to no avail.*

# Explosive Turn of Events

## Saturday, February 11, 1950

Arthur "Edward" Ferris, a World War II veteran, graduated Duke University in pre-med and was a third-year medical student when he dropped out. In the winter of '50 he was working at Dubs Sandwich Company in Durham and lived over on Minerva Avenue. He liked walking in the woods.

On this Saturday, he put on his army field jacket for warmth and hitchhiked over to the Highway 70 Bridge over the Eno east of Hillsborough. Ferris began walking back to Durham along the river about 3:00 p.m., not giving himself a lot of time before winter darkness set in. About an hour into his hike, as he strolled through the forest, Ferris first kicked and then saw a strange object beneath a cluster of leaves. Stooping to brush off the leaves, he bent down to pick it up. Examining the object, it exploded in a devastating blast to his hand and face.

Fragments blinded Ferris in both eyes. His face was pitted with powder burns. His right thumb was mangled, and zinc-covered wire embedded in one eye, his arm and the sleeve of his jacket. After the initial shock wore off, Ferris went into survival mode. He had a pistol with him and fired it hoping to draw attention and badly needed help. No one responded. In 1950, this area of the Eno was a vast wilderness and north Durham miles away. Ferris wandered blindly for five hours before finding the highway again. He came out near John Micol's farm, just west of the Durham County line, five miles from where he was injured.

Ferris was blindly groping in the middle of the dark road at ten after eight when a carload of Duke medical students found him. Their first impression was Ferris was drunk, and they feared he would be hit by a car. Stopping to check him out, they found him drenched in blood. They put him in the car and drove him to Duke Hospital. There he was listed in serious condition. Three days later, the hospital upgraded him to fair condition with a fifty-fifty chance of saving the left eye. A month later, it was still unknown if he would regain vision. There was no saving the right eye. The right thumb required amputation.

Durham and Orange County officers, under the leadership of Durham Sheriff E.G. "Cat" Belvin, went out on Valentine's Day searching the area but failed to find the explosion site. They were unsuccessful when they tried again the next day. Sheriff Belvin didn't discount the possibility that the story was fabricated and Ferris injured himself with a homemade bomb or grenade. Still, he continued the search "because we want to uncover all the clues we can to the thing that almost killed a man."

Ferris's mother and father came down from New York City to be with him during his recovery. We are pleased to report Ferris healed and lived another fifty-nine years. The bomb site was never found.

# ABOUT OUR STORYTELLER

Dave Cook was a North Carolina State Park ranger for thirty years at five different locations. Sixteen years were as the superintendent of the Eno River State Park. The last three years were as a district superintendent, of which Eno River was one of nine parks he supported. After retiring from state parks, he spent more than four years as the Eno River Association Education and Outreach coordinator. His first exposure to the Eno was camping there as a Boy Scout. He still frequents all the Eno River parks. All stories told in first person are from our author's personal experiences.

*Visit us at*
www.historypress.com